Common Core State Standards for Grade 6

Also by the Author

Common Core State Standards for Grades K–1: Language Arts Instructional Strategies and Activities

Common Core State Standards for Grades 2–3: Language Arts Instructional Strategies and Activities

Common Core State Standards for Grades 4–5: Language Arts Instructional Strategies and Activities

Common Core State Standards for Grade 6

Language Arts Instructional Strategies and Activities

Michelle Manville

ROWMAN & LITTLEFIELD
Lanham • Boulder • New York • London

Published by Rowman & Littlefield
A wholly owned subsidiary of The Rowman & Littlefield Publishing Group, Inc.
4501 Forbes Boulevard, Suite 200, Lanham, Maryland 20706
www.rowman.com

16 Carlisle Street, London W1D 3BT, United Kingdom

Copyright © 2014 by Michelle Manville

All rights reserved. No part of this book may be reproduced in any form or by any electronic or mechanical means, including information storage and retrieval systems, without written permission from the publisher, except by a reviewer who may quote passages in a review.

British Library Cataloguing in Publication Information Available

Library of Congress Cataloging-in-Publication Data

Manville, Michelle, 1953–
 Common core state standards for grade 6 : language arts instructional strategies and activities / Michelle Manville.
   pages cm
 Includes bibliographical references.
 ISBN 978-1-4758-1015-8 (pbk. : alk. paper)—ISBN 978-1-4758-1016-5 (electronic) 1. Language arts (Elementary)—Curricula—United States—States. 2. Language arts (Elementary)—Standards—United States—States. I. Title.
 LB1576.M3776 2014
 372.6—dc23
 2014003637

∞™ The paper used in this publication meets the minimum requirements of American National Standard for Information Sciences Permanence of Paper for Printed Library Materials, ANSI/NISO Z39.48-1992.

Printed in the United States of America

Contents

Introduction   vii

1	Instructional Strategies and Activities: An Overview	1
2	Grade 6 Common Core State Standards	13
3	Grades 6–8 Text Exemplars	23
4	Grade 6 Strategies and Activities for Reading Literature	27
5	Grade 6 Strategies and Activities for Reading Informational Text	51
6	Grade 6 Strategies and Activities for Writing	61
7	Grade 6 Strategies and Activities for Speaking and Listening	75
8	Grade 6 Strategies and Activities for Language	81
9	Grade 6 Strategies and Activities for Reading Literacy in History and Social Studies	85
10	Grade 6 Strategies and Activities for Reading Literacy in Science and Technical Subjects	95
11	Grade 6 Strategies and Activities for Writing in History, Social Studies, Science, and Technical Subjects	107

Appendix A: Summary Frames	115
Appendix B: Position Paper Format	117
Appendix C: Stem Questions	119
Appendix D: Hypothesis Worksheet	121
Appendix E: Primary Source Analysis	123
Appendix F: Sample Grade 6 Advance Organizers	125
Appendix G: Sample Parent Letter	127
Appendix H: Products and Performances	129
Appendix I: Verbs to Question	131
References	135
About the Author	137

Introduction

The Common Core State Standards for English Language Arts and Literacy in History/Social Studies, Science, and Technical Subjects were developed to ensure that students are ready for the challenges of college and career literacy by the end of their high school years. The standards were developed around K–12 grade-specific areas of reading literature and informational text, writing, speaking and listening, and language. These research- and evidence-based standards are rigorous and are aligned to the College and Career Readiness anchor standards, which establish what all students should know and be able to do upon entering postsecondary institutions.

At a time when schools across the nation are looking for ways to improve student achievement in most content areas, it seems reasonable to combine the standards and effective instructional strategies as you create activities to help with the implementation of the Common Core State Standards (CCSS).

When you look at the CCSS, think of the standards as representative of what students need to know and be able to do and what you need to do as a teacher to help them be successful. Based on the identified CCSS and other skills, students need to know how to compare and contrast, summarize information and take notes, create visual representations of information, work together collaboratively, conduct research, and be able to ask and answer higher-order questions. Additionally, to help students achieve success, teachers need to provide ample opportunities to practice new skills and demonstrate and enhance new learning.

A multitude of studies have been conducted over the past thirty years. From these studies, Education Northwest, formerly Northwest Regional Education Laboratory (2005), compiled a list of effective instructional strategies with descriptions, research findings, and implementation suggestions. When developing activities to address CCSS, keep in mind the strategies of identifying similarities and differences, summarizing and note taking, nonlinguistic representations, cooperative learning, generating and testing hypotheses, questions, cues, and advanced organizers, and homework and practice. As teachers, provide many opportunities for homework and practice as you implement the CCSS.

There's no guarantee that activities based on any strategy will help in every instance, and it may be quite possible that some strategies are more effective in certain subject areas and grade levels and with students from different backgrounds and aptitudes. Whether or not you use a strategy will depend on your students' previous knowledge and current abilities.

It is the intent of this book to give teachers a ready-made resource to use when planning lessons around CCSS. In each section you will find grade-appropriate, ready-to-use activities aligned to specific CCSS in English Language Arts and Literacy in History/Social Studies, Science, and Technical Subjects. All you need to supply is the content-rich text.

It is my hope that you will find this an essential component of your instructional materials as you plan your curriculum for the students of the twenty-first century.

ONE
Instructional Strategies and Activities: An Overview

Many of the Common Core State Standards (CCSS) can be taught and reinforced using a variety of activities combined with CCSS and effective instructional strategies. According to Visual Teaching Alliance (VTA; www.visualteachingalliance.com), "approximately 65 percent of the population are visual learners" and "90 percent of the information that comes to the brain is visual." The VTA also states that "the brain processes visual information 60,000 times faster than text" and that "visual aids in the classroom improve learning by up to 400 percent."

The use of graphic organizers—visuals—enables students to better organize their thinking and gives a visual frame of reference for information. Students are able to see the connections between previous learning and new knowledge. Graphic organizers increase students' abilities to use higher-order thinking skills, facilitate retention of information, are very brain friendly, and appeal to the multiple intelligences of visual-spatial, verbal-linguistic, logical-mathematical, and naturalist. The use of graphic organizers also helps those students who are English as a second language (ESL) or English language (EL) learners comprehend concepts more easily as there are fewer words to comprehend.

When you write lesson plans, think about the various graphic organizers you can use in activities: T-charts, Venn diagrams, matrices, concept maps, word webs, mind maps, graphs, chains, flow charts, and lists. Several suggestions are given throughout this book, but you may find a different organizer to help you help your students link new information to old or organize thoughts. Not all organizers are age or grade appropriate so choose carefully.

For those standards that are not appropriate for graphic organizers, you will find suggestions for a wide variety of structures that you can use in your classrooms. The ideas you find do not represent a definitive list and you may adapt those suggestions to use in other instances.

The instructional strategies described on the next few pages have been identified as effective practices by various educational practitioners based on a multitude of research. *Common Core State Standards for Grade 6: Language Arts Instructional Strategies and Activities* addresses the use of these strategies with respect to the K–12 CCSS for English Language Arts and Literacy in History/Social Studies, Science, and Technical Subjects and provides a multitude of ready-to-use activities.

SIMILARITIES AND DIFFERENCES

When students identify similarities and differences, the process helps students deepen the understanding of what they are learning. According to Markman and Gentner (1996), identifying similarities and differences is a basic cognitive process. Students use the processes of comparing, classifying, creating metaphors, and creating analogies to describe how items, events, processes, or concepts are similar or different. Comparison and/or contrast activities help students to better comprehend new concepts and allows the connection of new knowledge to existing concepts.

Teachers should not only point out similarities and differences to students, but should also allow students to develop their own strategies for comparing similarities and differences (http://netc.org/focus/strategies/iden.php). Students in Grade 6 should also describe *how* compared elements are different. T-charts and Venn diagrams are effective tools for teachers and students to identify similarities and differences. Matrices can also illustrate these concepts.

Grade 6 Activities

Activities to identify similarities and differences include creating T-charts, two- and three-circle Venn diagrams, organizational charts, classification charts, lists, graphs, maps, summary frames, essays, short research projects, opinion writing, creating analogies, mind maps, or word webs.

SUMMARIZING AND TAKING NOTES

Summarizing occurs unconsciously for most of us; yet, ask a student to write a summary of a chapter or a story and he or she may complain it is too difficult. We need to teach students to give us only the important details—eliminating the trivialities not necessary for comprehension. Valerie Anderson and Suzanne Hidi synthesized various research on summarization. According to Anderson and Hidi (1998/1999), when you first begin teaching summarization, be sure to choose short excerpts with easy text, such as narratives or texts with familiar concepts and ideas. Anderson and Hidi (1998/1999) also indicate that students need to be able to select or delete what is included and then reduce the information into a manageable amount.

Summary Frames

The use of summary frames helps students select and reduce information for summaries using specific questions and helps students develop a deeper comprehension of the information read. A summary frame is an effective structure when summarizing reading assignments. Studies by Meyer and Freedle (1984) show that reading comprehension increases when students learn how to incorporate summary frames. Summary frames also help students to focus on important information and allow teachers to determine the depth of comprehension through student responses.

Narrative or story frames include information about the characters, setting, actions, feelings, goals of the main character, and the consequences.

Definition frames use four questions: What concept is being defined? To which category does the item belong? What are the attributes or characteristics of the concept? What examples are given to illustrate the concept?

Problem-solution frames introduce a problem and identify one or more solutions following this format: statement of something that happened or might happen that could be problematic; a description of a solution; statements of other possible solutions; identification of a solution with the greatest chance of success.

Questions in an argumentation frame are centered on the information that leads to a claim, the basic statement of focus, examples that support the claim, and concessions made about the claim. You will need to know the abilities of your students to begin using the argumentation frame effectively in your classroom.

Grade 6 Activities

Common summarization activities for Grade 6 include the use of narrative or story, definition and problem-solution summary frames, acrostics, journal entries, visual representations (bulletin boards, posters, models), concept webs, multicolumn T-charts, concept webs, timelines, outlines, 5W and How charts, raps or other songs, mnemonics, and paraphrases. See Appendix A for examples of summary frames.

Taking Notes

The concept of taking notes in class used to imply writing every important word one could remember as quickly as possible or copying the teacher's words from the blackboard, whiteboard, or overhead projector. If we all had photographic memories, then there would be no reason to take notes. However, that is not the case. The good news is that students can be taught how to summarize information and take good notes.

Verbatim notes are the least effective way of taking notes in a classroom setting and are not conducive to selecting and reducing, which is key to taking good notes. When copying the teacher's words, students are not engaged in the information except to the extent that they write down every word. Very little, if anything, is committed to long- or even short-term memory. Students must identify the key information they are learning about and put it into their own words.

Taking notes is very personal in style, but students need to be taught various formats to enable them to choose the style that best suits their tastes and needs. Teachers should model good note-taking formats. Begin with outlines of information you are going to present. Impress upon students that reviewing and revising notes can lead to a deeper understanding of the information presented and will help the students to make the information their own (Anderson & Armbruster, 1986).

Grade 6 Activities

Activities to teach note taking include creating graphic organizers, outlines, note cards, paraphrases, mnemonic devices, concept maps, flashcards, two-column notes, flowcharts, multicolumn charts, and diagrams. Other activities include reading or taking notes outside or in a special place in the classroom, using content-related visuals in the classroom, and creating songs or pictures that represent key concepts.

NONLINGUISTIC REPRESENTATIONS

When students use nonlinguistic representations in activities, they use words, pictures, and symbols to convey knowledge while learning. The use of this strategy helps students synthesize information in a way that makes sense to them and are then better able to retain and recall the information. In most classroom applications, students and teachers will combine words in graphic organizers with the nonlinguistic representations. The use of visual representations helps students recognize how concepts are connected (National Council of Teachers of Mathematics, 2000).

There are many examples of mind maps or webs or pictorial representations you can use in the classroom. You may have to teach students how to create these representations. Kagan and Kagan (1997) offer these helpful hints when creating mind maps: "use white space, practice symbols and images, emphasize important images, and practice." Students can also create pictographs that use representative pictures or symbols to present information.

The brain is a pattern-seeking device; nonlinguistic representations are patterns. Use of these patterns can help most all students, especially the visual-spatial student, comprehend and retain information. The use of patterns helps students organize their thinking and helps them apply what they have learned (Bransford et al., 1999; Lehrer & Chazen, 1998).

Nonlinguistic representation activities create visuals, and according to Lehrer and Chazen (1998, p. 6), "by ignoring visualization, curricula not only fail to engage a powerful part of students' minds in service of their mathematical thinking, but also fail to develop students' skills at visual exploration and argument." The ability to visualize can also serve the language arts student as well.

Grade 6 Activities

To create activities using nonlinguistic representations, include role-playing and dramatizations such as plays or skits, puppet shows, or press conferences; create murals, brochures, bulletin boards, posters, or scenic backdrops; illustrate favorite parts of stories or poems or create bookmarks or book covers; participate in kinesthetic activities; produce oral readings, recordings, narrations and recitations; listen to commercially produced CDs or student recordings; create physical models such as dioramas or representative artifacts; and draw and create other pictorial representations such as illustrated webs, murals, dioramas, trifolds, scrapbooks, posters, T-shirts, book jackets or bookmarks, mind maps, travel brochures, and PowerPoint presentations.

COOPERATIVE LEARNING

A graphic attributed to American psychologist William Glasser, based on a graphic created by Edgar Dale (1969, p. 108), indicates this: We learn 10 percent of what we read, 20 percent of what we hear, 30 percent of what we see, 50 percent of what we see and hear, 70 percent of what we discuss, 80 percent of what we experience, and 95 percent of what we teach to others. Perhaps an easier way to describe Glasser's view of learning would be to say "two heads are better than one."

What Is Cooperative Learning?

Cooperative learning is *not* group work. It *is* where two or more students work together cooperatively to achieve a common goal. According to Johnson and Johnson (1999, as cited in Education Northwest, formerly Northwest Regional Educational Laboratory, 2005, para. 1) "effective cooperative learning occurs when students work together to accomplish shared goals and when positive structures are in place to support that process." Students in Grade 6 should continue to work with others as the concept of cooperative learning is a lifelong lesson that will help them throughout their lives.

Teachers and students alike are often placed into group settings where either everyone or no one is in charge; where chaos reigns; where nothing is accomplished. Unless you know how to work in a group, the group is almost certainly doomed. When groups work within specific guidelines, then the group allows for more student interaction, inquiry thinking, time-on-task, in-depth questions, and student accountability. Shy students will feel safe. Studies show that cooperative learning enhances student performance and should not be based on competition.

A Teacher's Role in Cooperative Learning

The teacher's role in cooperative learning includes selecting the group size, assignment of students to the groups, arranging the classroom, providing appropriate materials, setting the task and goal structure, monitoring student-student interaction, intervening to solve problems and teach skills, and evaluating the outcomes (Johnson & Johnson, 1999).

Sometimes teachers will want to assign specific roles to specific students or you may want to give a list of possible roles to students and let them work it out. You will always want to make sure that roles rotate among the students. The number of roles you have will obviously depend on the number of students in a group and the nature of the work to be done in the group. You might want to create roles such as: leader, recorder or secretary, checker, speaker, facilitator, timekeeper, summarizer, and reflector (http://serc.carleton.edu/introgeo/cooperative/roles.html).

Grade 6 Activities

Cooperative learning activities for Grade 6 include the Kagan Cooperative Learning (Kagan & Kagan, 1997) structures of Think-Pair-Share, Paraphrase Passport, and Jigsaw. Other activities include peer editing and revising, conducting group research, publishing, collaborative discussions, and group presentations.

GENERATING AND TESTING HYPOTHESES

Students must learn to question in order to question to learn. Students who are able to generate and test their hypotheses—ask questions and explain their hypotheses—will greatly enhance their own learning. Children begin to ask questions as soon as they begin talking and continue to ask questions through adulthood. Teachers can help students learn to ask good questions which will help them make better hypotheses. Students who are able to explain their hypotheses will demonstrate their understanding of concepts as well.

Research Findings

According to Lavoie and Good (1998) and Lawson (1998, as cited in Education Northwest, formerly Northwest Regional Educational Laboratory 2005, para. 3) "understanding increases when students are asked to explain the scientific principles they are working from and the hypotheses they generate from these principles."

Similarly, White and Frederickson (1998, as cited in Education Northwest, formerly Northwest Regional Educational Laboratory 2005, para. 5) found that when comparing "inquiry-based instruction and traditional teaching methods (such as lectures and textbook-based instruction), researchers found that inquiry methods helped students gain a better understanding of fundamental science concepts." These ideas can be applied to language arts, too.

Applications for Language Arts Classrooms

The ability to generate and test hypotheses isn't just for science anymore. For example, a language arts teacher could ask students to read literature, predict the actions of one or more of the characters, and then read and discuss the accuracy of the predictions (Kuhn, 2009). Leach (2010) describes how teachers show students various pictures dealing with short stories or novels they are reading and how teachers ask students to predict the outcome of events based on the pictures.

Students can predict the ending of a story at the middle of the book and discuss the accuracy of their hypotheses at the end. Other ways to generate and test hypotheses include learning about a debatable historical event and hypothesizing about the actual events, reading two or more books to test the hypothesis; brainstorming techniques that persuade people in debate and hypothesizing which techniques work best; and finally, talking about how characters in a novel react and hypothesizing about how students would react in the same situation, checking with several to test the hypothesis (Janel W., 2009).

Seize the opportunity to use the natural curiosity of all students. They love to question why we do things, so turn it around on them and let them discover why and what. Teach students the art of asking strong, higher-order questions, and challenge them to explain the results of their findings.

Grade 6 Activities

Classroom activities for generating and testing hypotheses in Grade 6 include asking students to make and test hypotheses, make predictions, solve problems, conduct historical investigations, make observations, and make decisions based on information. See Appendix C for stem questions and Appendix I for lists of higher- and lower-order verbs.

QUESTIONS, CUES, AND ADVANCE ORGANIZERS

The brain as a pattern-seeking device looks to link new information to previous knowledge. When we use cues, questions and advance organizers, we access what students already know and prepare them for what they are about to learn.

Research Findings

Marzano et al. (2001, p. 113) found (as cited in Davis & Tinsley, 1967; Fillippone, 1998) that "cueing and questioning might account for as much as 80 percent of what occurs in a given classroom on a given day." If we are asking that many questions, then we need to consider the quality of the questions we ask. Are we asking questions that reflect the most important content? Do we ask higher-order questions or do we simply ask students to recall information?

Redfield and Rousseau (1981) found that asking higher-level questions, rather than asking recall questions, requires students to analyze information which results in more learning. Do teachers tend to ask more lower-order questions? Do we use questions, cues, and advance organizers to focus learning? Are we waiting long enough for students to give more thoughtful responses? Do we give some students longer to respond because of who they are? T. W. Fowler (1975) found that when teachers are taught a technique related to the amount of wait time after asking a question, students are more likely to participate and participate more frequently in small group student-to-student interactions.

Determine the Types of Questions Asked

One way to determine the types of questions you use in the classroom is to audio record several instructional sessions in your classroom. This will give you the opportunity to hear how much wait time you give and to whom. Using the "Verbs to Question" page in Appendix I, mark the verbs you use in your class. If you use more lower-order verbs in instruction, then use more higher-order verbs. If you teach more than one content area, you might want to record various content areas and see what types of questions you ask. Maybe there is a correlation to the content area where you ask the higher- or lower-order questions.

You can also create a list of higher-order, grade-appropriate verbs and post them in your classroom. You may wish to choose verbs from Appendix I. When you use K-W-L charts, use the list to help improve the questions on your chart. If we do not use higher-order questions in our classroom instruction, then we cannot expect students to ask them either.

Use Cues and Questions

Cues are hints or reminders that help access prior knowledge and are generally explicit in nature. In the book *Checking for Understanding: Formative Assessment Techniques for Your Classroom*, Douglas Fisher and Nancy Frey (2007) suggest teachers use symbols, words, or phrases to help students recall information. Fisher and Frey (2007) also suggest using direct eye contact, facial expressions, body posture, physical distance, silence, short verbal acknowledgments, and sub-summaries (restating or paraphrasing main ideas).

Questions can act as cues or require students to analyze information. Questions should engage students in their learning and increase participation in the classroom. Fisher and Frey (2007) identified several strategies that are helpful in questioning. These strategies include response cards, hand signals, and audience response systems.

Advance Organizers

Sometimes you need more than a cue or question. Use advance organizers when introducing new concepts as they will help link previous knowledge to the new learning that is going to take place. Advance organizers are organizational frameworks that provide guidance as to the important information in a lesson or unit. Information that is presented graphically and symbolically reinforces reading and learning skills (Brookbank et al., 1999).

Grade 6 Activities

When creating Grade 6 activities around questions, cues, and advance organizers, include the use of higher-order questions, using visual cues and advance organizers such as narrative frames, timelines, and webs. See Appendix F for sample Grade 6 Advance Organizers.

HOMEWORK AND PRACTICE

Thomas Edison once said that "genius is 2 percent inspiration and 98 percent perspiration" and he felt that hard work would get one to the "top rung of Fortune's ladder" (Jones, 1908, p. 347). It is up to us to make homework and practice meaningful to students so that their 98 percent perspiration will help them become the geniuses they can be. Create a variety of activities that enable students to practice the CCSS skills.

Homework activities should not be busy work. The activities should have a purpose that is clearly articulated to students. In the book *Rethinking Homework: Best Practices That Support Diverse Needs*, Cathy Vatterott (2009) suggests that homework be given to help the learning process in four ways: prelearning, checking for understanding, practice, and processing. It is important to prepare students for new content and for teachers to find out what students already know about the content.

Additionally, "Students should easily understand the value of the task or be told explicitly how it [homework] helps learning" (Vatterott, 2009, p. 100). Give students specific reasons for the day's homework either in writing on the assignment itself or verbally. Use phrases such as "Today's homework will allow you to practice previous knowledge or new skills"; "Reflect on learning"; "Review for tests or quizzes"; and "check for understanding of concepts" (Vatterott, 2009).

There is an old adage that says "practice makes perfect." However, many believe practice makes better and that only perfect practice makes perfect. The very essence of homework is to provide such practice, especially for rote skills—alphabet, multiplication tables, the names of all the state capitals in the United States. But if students do not understand a concept and teachers do not check for understanding, then the practice could lead to misconceptions and inaccurate learning.

Thomas Armstrong (2006, p. 129) suggests teachers "link [homework] in some way to the feelings, memories, or personal associations of the students" with words such as "think of a time in your life when you." Whenever you connect the curriculum to students in such a manner, you create an emotionally meaningful attachment between the student and the curriculum.

Research Findings and Recommendations

According to Harris Cooper (1989, p. 89), "It is better to distribute material across several assignments rather than have homework concentrate only on material covered in class that day." Students need to process new information as they link it to previous knowledge. Processing is where students reflect on concepts by considering specific questions to ask, applying information learned, and making connections to a bigger picture (Vatterott, 2009).

You will also want to consider the amount of homework and practice activities at each grade level. Recommendations from various studies by the Pennsylvania Department of Education (1973), Bond and Smith (1966), and Strang (1975) (as cited in Marzano et al., 2001) for total minutes of homework per day vary from forty to ninety minutes for upper elementary. Other schools of thought use the "ten-minute rule" to establish optimum homework amounts. Cooper ("Duke Study: Homework," 2006) described it as ten minutes of homework per grade level. Additional studies show that about every thirty minutes of "additional" homework a student does per night her grade point average increases about a half a point (Keith & Cool, 1992).

In her article "The War on Homework," Bea McGarvey (2007, p. 6) "advised educators to ask how homework supports the knowledge they want students to learn." She also asks teachers to look at their grade books to see if they are tracking assignments or attainment of learning goals. Are your homework and practice activities geared toward learning or keeping students busy?

Suggestions for Parents

For those parents who absolutely "must" help, give them a list of "helpful activities" in which they can participate without jeopardizing procedures and processes you have established and content you have taught in class. A good time to share tips with parents could be at an open house or back-to-school night. Teachers could also include a list of tips in registration packets that may be handed or sent out just before the new school year.

How should middle school parents help their children with homework? Parents can help the child find a quiet location to do homework; establish a sense of organization by creating a homework supply box that contains paper, pens, pencils, tape, glue, dictionary/thesaurus, calculator, markers, rulers, and other necessary items; establish a time or schedule for homework; have a positive attitude about the homework; and check it for completion and understanding.

Parents can work with students to create mnemonics to help remember key details. Prepare Q&As—where a parent creates questions over the material and the student reads to find the answers. Encourage parents to participate in "quick writes" where the student reads or reviews small chunks of notes or material and then shares, either verbally or in writing on sticky notes, any key details. The parent can check the notes or material for accuracy, and the student can add the sticky notes to the study materials. Students can use their notes and other materials to "teach" concepts to parents.

Students can share their homework assignments with their parents so the students see that parents value the time and effort and learning that go along with homework. When students see that the work they do is valued, then possibly they are more inclined to do better work.

Grade 6 Activities

Homework and practice activities for Grade 6 include summary frames, advertisements, museum exhibits, recitations, quiz shows, flashcards, webs, journal writing, scavenger hunts, Venn diagrams, charts and graphs, timelines, speeches, scrapbooks, news stories, letters to authors or speakers, keyboarding skills, various forms of writing, Q&A sessions, bio-poems, research projects, read-alouds, note cards, news stories and headlines, poetry, storyboards, concept webs, and many others. See Appendix G for a sample parent letter.

LET'S GET STARTED!

Now you have an overview of various instructional strategies and activities to use with the Grade 6 CCSS. The rest of the book is devoted to specific activities to use with the strands of reading literature, reading informational text, writing, speaking and listening, and language. You also have strategies and activities for reading literacy and writing in history, social studies, science, and technical subjects. Within each strand you will find many ready-to-use grade level appropriate activities aligned to specific standards. Many activities will incorporate other standards as well.

You will also find a list of the grade level text exemplars; you are not expected to use the exemplars, but if you have them in your classroom, use them. There are many other wonderful, grade-appropriate books for you and your students to use if the exemplars are not available to you. Other selections are suggested within the activities.

I hope you find this a valuable tool as you implement the CCSS in your classroom.

TWO
Grade 6 Common Core State Standards

READING LITERATURE

- RL.6.1—Cite textual evidence to support analysis of what the text says explicitly as well as inferences drawn from the text.
- RL.6.2—Determine a theme or central idea of a text and how it is conveyed through particular details; provide a summary of the text distinct from personal opinions or judgments.
- RL.6.3—Describe how a particular story's or drama's plot unfolds in a series of episodes as well as how the characters respond or change as the plot moves toward a resolution.
- RL.6.4—Determine the meaning of words and phrases as they are used in a text, including figurative and connotative meanings; analyze the impact of a specific word choice on meaning and tone.
- RL.6.5—Analyze how a particular sentence, chapter, scene, or stanza fits into the overall structure of a text and contributes to the development of the theme, setting or plot.
- RL.6.6—Explain how an author develops the point of view of the narrator or speaker in a text.
- RL.6.7—Compare and contrast the experience of reading a story, drama, or poem to listening to or viewing an audio, video, or live version of the text, including contrasting what they "see" and "hear" when reading the text to what they perceive when they listen or watch.
- RL.6.9—Compare and contrast texts in different forms or genres (e.g., stories and poems, historical novels and fantasy stories) in terms of their approaches to similar themes and topics.

- RL.6.10—By the end of the year, read and comprehend literature, including stories, dramas, and poems, in the Grades 6–8 text complexity band proficiently, with scaffolding as needed at the high end of the range.

READING INFORMATIONAL TEXT

- RI.6.1—Cite textual evidence to support analysis of what the text says explicitly as well as inferences drawn from the text.
- RI.6.2—Determine a central idea of a text and how it is conveyed through particular details; provide a summary of the text distinct from personal opinions or judgments.
- RI.6.3—Analyze in detail how a key individual, event, or idea is introduced, illustrated, and elaborated in a text (e.g., through examples or anecdotes).
- RI.6.4—Determine the meaning of words and phrases as they are used in a text, including figurative, connotative, and technical meanings.
- RI.6.5—Analyze how a particular sentence, paragraph, chapter, or section fits into the overall structure of a text and contributes to the development of the ideas.
- RI.6.6—Determine an author's point of view or purpose in a text and explain how it is conveyed in the text.
- RI.6.7—Integrate information presented in different media or formats (e.g., visually, quantitatively) as well as in words to develop a coherent understanding of a topic or issue.
- RI.6.8—Trace and evaluate the argument and specific claims in a text, distinguishing claims that are supported by reasons and evidence from claims that are not.
- RI.6.9—Compare and contrast one author's presentation of events with that of another (e.g., a memoir written by and a biography on the same person).
- RI.6.10—By the end of the year, read and comprehend literary nonfiction in the Grades 6–8 text complexity band proficiently, with scaffolding as needed at the high end of the range.

WRITING

- W.6.1—Write arguments to support claims with clear reasons and relevant evidence.
- W.6.1a—Introduce claim(s) and organize the reasons and evidence clearly.

- W.6.1b—Support claim(s) with clear reasons and relevant evidence, using credible sources and demonstrating an understanding of the topic or text.
- W.6.1c—Use words, phrases, and clauses to clarify the relationships among claim(s) and reasons.
- W.6.1d—Establish and maintain a formal style.
- W.6.1e—Provide a concluding statement or section that follows from the argument presented.
- W.6.2—Write informative/explanatory texts to examine a topic and convey ideas, concepts, and information through the selection, organization, and analysis of relevant content.
- W.6.2a—Introduce a topic; organize ideas, concepts, and information, using strategies such as definition, classification, comparison/contrast and cause/effect; include formatting (e.g., headings), graphics (e.g., charts, tables), and multimedia when useful to aiding comprehension.
- W.6.2b—Develop a topic with relevant facts, definitions, concrete details, quotations, or other information and examples.
- W.6.2c—Use appropriate transitions to clarify the relationships among ideas and concepts.
- W.6.2d—Use precise language and domain-specific vocabulary to inform about or explain the topic.
- W.6.2e—Establish and maintain a formal style.
- W.6.2f—Provide a concluding statement or section that follows from the information or explanation presented.
- W.6.3—Write narratives to develop real or imagined experiences or events using effective technique, relevant descriptive details, and well-structured event sequences.
- W.6.3a—Engage and orient the reader by establishing a context and introducing a narrator and/or characters; organize an event sequence that unfolds naturally and logically.
- W.6.3b—Use narrative techniques, such as dialogue, pacing, and description, to develop experiences, events, and/or characters.
- W.6.3c—Use a variety of transition words, phrases, and clauses to convey sequence and signal shifts from one time frame or setting to another.
- W.6.3d—Use precise words and phrases, relevant descriptive details, and sensory language to convey experience and events.
- W.6.3e—Provide a conclusion that follows from the narrated experiences or events.
- W.6.4—Produce clear and coherent writing in which the development, organization, and style are appropriate to task, purpose, and audience.

- W.6.5—With some guidance and support from peers and adults, develop and strengthen writing as needed by planning, revising, editing, rewriting, or trying a new approach.
- W.6.6—Use technology, including the Internet, to produce and publish writing as well as to interact and collaborate with others; demonstrate sufficient command of keyboarding skills to type a minimum of three pages in a single sitting.
- W.6.7—Conduct short research projects to answer a question, drawing on several sources and refocusing the inquiry when appropriate.
- W.6.8—Gather relevant information from multiple print and digital sources, assess the credibility of each source, and quote or paraphrase the data and conclusions of others while avoiding plagiarism and providing basic bibliographic information for sources.
- W.6.9—Draw evidence from literary or informational texts to support analysis, reflection, and research.
- W.6.10—Write routinely over extended time frames (time for research, reflection, and revision) and shorter time frames (a single sitting or a day or two) for a range of discipline-specific tasks, purposes, and audiences.

SPEAKING AND LISTENING

- SL.6.1—Engage effectively in a range of collaborative discussions (one-on-one, in groups, and teacher-led) with diverse partners on Grade 6 topics, texts, and issues, building on others' ideas and expressing their own clearly.
- SL.6.1a—Come to discussions prepared, having read or studied required material; explicitly draw on that preparation by referring to evidence on the topic, text, or issue to probe and reflect on ideas under discussion.
- SL.6.1b—Follow rules for collegial discussions, set specific goals and deadlines, and define individual roles as needed.
- SL.6.1c—Pose and respond to specific questions with elaboration and detail by making comments that contribute to the topic, text, or issue under discussion.
- SL.6.1d—Review the key ideas expressed and demonstrate understanding of multiple perspectives through reflection and paraphrasing.
- SL.6.2—Interpret information presented in diverse media and formats (e.g., visually, quantitatively, orally) and explain how it contributes to a topic, text, or issue under study.

- SL.6.3—Delineate a speaker's argument and specific claims, distinguishing claims that are supported by reasons and evidence from claims that are not.
- SL.6.4—Present claims and findings, sequencing ideas logically and using pertinent descriptions, facts and details to accentuate main ideas or themes; use appropriate eye contact, adequate volume, and clear pronunciation.
- SL.6.5—Include multimedia components (e.g., graphics, images, music, sound) and visual displays in presentations to clarify information.
- SL.6.6—Adapt speech to a variety of contexts and tasks, demonstrating command of formal English when indicated or appropriate.

LANGUAGE

- L.6.1—Demonstrate command of the conventions of standard English grammar and usage when writing or speaking.
- L.6.1a—Ensure that pronouns are in the proper case (subjective, objective, possessive).
- L.6.1b—Use intensive pronouns (e.g., myself, ourselves).
- L.6.1c—Recognize and correct inappropriate shifts in pronoun number and person.
- L.6.1d—Recognize and correct vague pronouns (i.e., ones with unclear or ambiguous antecedents).
- L.6.1e—Recognize variations from standard English in their own and others' writing and speaking, and identify and use strategies to improve expression in conventional language.
- L.6.2—Demonstrate command of the conventions of standard English capitalization, punctuation, and spelling when writing.
- L.6.2a—Use punctuation (commas, parentheses, dashes) to set off nonrestrictive/parenthetical elements.
- L.6.2b—Spell correctly.
- L.6.3—Use knowledge of language and its conventions when writing, speaking, reading, or listening.
- L.6.3a—Vary sentence patterns for meaning, reader/listener interest, and style.
- L.6.3b—Maintain consistency in style and tone.
- L.6.4—Determine or clarify the meaning of unknown and multiple-meaning words and phrases based on Grade 6 reading and content, choosing flexibly from a range of strategies.
- L.6.4a—Use context (e.g., the overall meaning of a sentence or paragraph; a word's position or function in a sentence) as a clue to the meaning of a word or phrase.

- L.6.4b—Use common, grade-appropriate Greek or Latin affixes and roots as clues to the meaning of a word (e.g., audience, auditory, audible).
- L.6.4c—Consult reference materials (e.g., dictionaries, glossaries, thesauruses), both print and digital, to find the pronunciation of a word or determine or clarify its precise meaning or its part of speech.
- L.6.4d—Verify the preliminary determination of the meaning of a word or phrase (e.g., by checking the inferred meaning in context or in a dictionary).
- L.6.5—Demonstrate understanding of figurative language, word relationships, and nuances in word meanings.
- L.6.5a—Interpret figures of speech (e.g., personification) in context.
- L.6.5b—Use the relationship between particular words (e.g., cause/effect, part/whole, item/category) to better understand each of the words.
- L.6.5c—Distinguish among the connotations (associations) or words with similar denotations (definitions) (e.g., stingy, scrimping, economical, unwasteful, thrifty).
- L.6.6—Acquire and use accurately grade-appropriate general academic and domain-specific words and phrases; gather vocabulary knowledge when considering a word or phrase important to comprehension or expression.

READING LITERACY IN HISTORY/SOCIAL STUDIES

- RLHS.6-8.1—Cite textual evidence to support analysis of primary and secondary sources.
- RLHS.6-8.2—Determine the central ideas or information of a primary or secondary source; provide an accurate summary of the source distinct from prior knowledge or opinions.
- RLHS.6-8.3—Identify key steps in a text's description of a process related to history/social studies (e.g., how a bill becomes law, how interest rates are raised or lowered).
- RLHS.6-8.4—Determine the meaning of words and phrases as they are used in a text, including vocabulary specific to domains related to history/social studies.
- RLHS.6-8.5—Describe how a text presents information (e.g., sequentially, comparatively, causally).
- RLHS.6-8.6—Identify aspects of a text that reveal an author's point of view or purpose (e.g., loaded language, inclusion or avoidance of particular facts).

- RLHS.6-8.7—Integrate visual information (e.g., in charts, graphs, photographs, videos, or maps) with other information in print and digital texts.
- RLHS.6-8.8—Distinguish among fact, opinion, and reasoned judgment in a text.
- RLHS.6-8.9—Analyze the relationship between a primary and secondary source on the same topic.

READING LITERACY IN SCIENCE AND TECHNICAL SUBJECTS

- RLST.6-8.1—Cite specific textual evidence to support analysis of science and technical texts.
- RLST.6-8.2—Determine the central ideas or conclusions of a text; provide an accurate summary of the text distinct from prior knowledge or opinions.
- RLST.6-8.3—Follow precisely a multistep procedure when carrying out experiments, taking measurements, or performing technical tasks.
- RLST.6-8.4—Determine the meaning of symbols, key terms, and other domain-specific words and phrases as they are used in a specific scientific or technical context relevant to Grade 6 texts and topics.
- RLST.6-8.5—Analyze the structure an author uses to organize a text, including how the major sections contribute to the whole and to an understanding of the topic.
- RLST.6-8.6—Analyze the author's purpose in providing an explanation, describing a procedure or discussing an experiment in a text.
- RLST.6-8.7—Integrate quantitative or technical information expressed in words in a text with a version of that information expressed visually (e.g., in a flowchart, diagram, model, graph, or table).
- RLST.6-8.8—Distinguish among facts, reasoned judgment based on research findings, and speculation in a text.
- RLST.6-8.9—Compare and contrast the information gained from experiments, simulations, video, or multimedia sources with that gained from reading a text on the same topic.

WRITING LITERACY IN HISTORY/SOCIAL STUDIES, SCIENCE, AND TECHNICAL SUBJECTS

- WHST.6-8.1—Write arguments focused on discipline-specific content.

- WHST.6-8.1a — Introduce claim(s) about a topic or issue, acknowledge and distinguish the claim(s) from alternate or opposing claims, and organize the reasons and evidence logically.
- WHST.6-8.1b — Support claim(s) with logical reasoning and relevant, accurate data and evidence that demonstrate an understanding of the topic or text, using credible sources.
- WHST.6-8.1c — Use words, phrases, and clauses to create cohesion and clarify the relationships among claim(s), counterclaims, reasons, and evidence.
- WHST.6-8.1d — Establish and maintain a formal style.
- WHST.6-8.1e — Provide a concluding statement or section that follows from and supports the argument presented.
- WHST.6-8.2 — Write informative/explanatory texts, including the narration of historical events, scientific procedures/experiments, or technical processes.
- WHST.6-8.2a — Introduce a topic clearly, previewing what is to follow; organize ideas, concepts, and information into broader categories as appropriate to achieving purpose; include formatting (e.g., headings), graphics (e.g., charts, tables), and multimedia when useful to aiding comprehension.
- WHST.6-8.2b — Develop the topic with relevant, well-chosen facts, definitions, concrete details, quotations, or other information and examples.
- WHST.6-8.2c — Use appropriate and varied transitions to create cohesion and clarify the relationships among ideas and concepts.
- WHST.6-8.2d — Use precise language and domain-specific vocabulary to inform about or explain the topic.
- WHST.6-8.2e — Establish and maintain a formal style and objective tone.
- WHST.6-8.2f — Provide a concluding statement or section that follows from and supports the information or explanation presented.
- WHST.6-8.4 — Provide clear and coherent writing in which the development, organization, and style are appropriate to task, purpose, and audience.
- WHST.6-8.5 — With some guidance and support from peers and adults, develop and strengthen writing as needed by planning, revising, editing, rewriting, or trying a new approach, focusing on how well purpose and audience have been addressed.
- WHST.6-8.6 — Use technology, including the Internet, to produce and publish writing and present the relationships between information and ideas clearly and efficiently.
- WHST.6-8.7 — Conduct short research projects to answer a question (including a self-generated question), drawing on several sources and generating additional related, focused questions that allow for multiple avenues of exploration.

- WHST.6-8.8—Gather relevant information from multiple print and digital sources, using search terms effectively; assess the credibility and accuracy of each source; and quote or paraphrase the data and conclusions of others while avoiding plagiarism and following a standard format for citation.
- WHST.6-8.9—Draw evidence from informational texts to support analysis, reflection, and research.
- WHST.6-8.10—Write routinely over extended time frames (time for reflection and revision) and shorter time frames (a single sitting or a day or two) for a range of discipline-specific tasks, purposes, and audiences.

NOTE

A complete list of text standards, exemplars, and resource materials as identified by the National Governors Association Center for Best Practices can be found at http://corestandards.org/ELA-Literacy.

THREE
Grades 6–8 Text Exemplars

STORIES

Alcott, Louisa May. *Little Women*
Cisneros, Sandra. "Eleven"
Cooper, Susan. *The Dark Is Rising*
Hamilton, Virginia. "The People Could Fly"
L'Engle, Madeleine. *A Wrinkle in Time*
Paterson, Katherine. *The Tale of the Mandarin Ducks*
Sutcliff, Rosemary. *Black Ships before Troy: The Story of the Iliad*
Taylor, Mildred D. *Roll of Thunder, Hear My Cry*
Twain, Mark. *The Adventures of Tom Sawyer*
Yep, Laurence. *Dragonwings*

DRAMA

Fletcher, Louise. *Sorry, Wrong Number*
Goodrich, Frances, and Albert Hackett. *The Diary of Anne Frank: A Play*

POETRY

Carroll, Lewis. "Jabberwocky"
Dickinson, Emily. "The Railway Train"
Frost, Robert. "The Road Not Taken"
Giovanni, Nikki. "A Poem for My Librarian, Mrs. Long"
Hughes, Langston. "I, Too, Sing America"
Longfellow, Henry Wadsworth. "Paul Revere's Ride"
Navajo tradition. "Twelfth Song of Thunder"

Neruda, Pablo. "The Book of Questions"
Sandburg, Carl. "Chicago"
Soto, Gary. "Oranges"
Whitman, Walt. "O Captain, My Captain"
Yeats, William Butler. "The Song of Wandering Aengus"

INFORMATIONAL TEXTS: ENGLISH LANGUAGE ARTS

Adams, John. "Letter on Thomas Jefferson"
Churchill, Winston. "Blood, Toil, Tears and Sweat: Address to Parliament on May 13th, 1940"
Douglass, Frederick. *Narrative of the Life of Frederick Douglass an American Slave, Written by Himself*
Petry, Ann. *Harriet Tubman: Conductor on the Underground Railroad*
Steinbeck, John. *Travels with Charley: In Search of America*

INFORMATIONAL TEXTS: HISTORY/SOCIAL STUDIES

Freedman, Russell. *Freedom Walkers: The Story of the Montgomery Bus Boycott*
Greenberg, Jan, and Sandra Jordan. *Vincent Van Gogh: Portrait of an Artist*
Isaacson, Phillip. *A Short Walk through the Pyramids and through the World of Art*
Lord, Walter. *A Night to Remember*
Monk, Linda R. *Words We Live By: Your Annotated Guide to the Constitution*
Murphy, Jim. *The Great Fire*
Partridge, Elizabeth. *This Land Was Made for You and Me: The Life and Songs of Woody Guthrie*
United States Preamble and First Amendment to the United States Constitution (1787, 1791)

INFORMATIONAL TEXTS: SCIENCE,
MATHEMATICS, AND TECHNICAL SUBJECTS

California Invasive Plant Council. *Invasive Plant Inventory*
"Elementary Particles," *New Book of Popular Science*
Enzensberger, Hans Magnus. *The Number Devil: A Mathematical Adventure*
"Geology," *U*X*L Encyclopedia of Science*
Katz, John. *Geeks: How Two Lost Boys Rode the Internet Out of Idaho*
Macaulay, David. *Cathedral: The Story of Its Construction*

Mackay, Donald. *The Building of Manhattan*

Peterson, Ivars, and Nancy Henderson. *Math Trek: Adventures in the Math Zone*

Petroski, Henry. "The Evolution of the Grocery Bag"

"Space Probe," *Astronomy and Space: From the Big Bang to the Big Crunch*

NOTE

A complete list of text standards, exemplars, and resource materials as identified by the National Governors Association Center for Best Practices can be found at http://corestandards.org/ELA-Literacy.

FOUR
Grade 6 Strategies and Activities for Reading Literature

Choose literary text from Grades 6–8 text exemplars selections or other grade-level appropriate selections. Grades 6–8 exemplars are noted with an (EX). Other appropriate grade level selections include, but are not limited to, the following:

REALISTIC FICTION

Al Capone Does My Shirts by Gennifer Choldenko (2006)
Anne of Green Gables by Lucy Maud Montgomery (2004)
Baseball in April by Gary Soto (2000)
The Candymakers by Wendy Mass (2011)
Close to Famous by Joan Bauer (2012)
Diary of a Wimpy Kid by Jeff Kinney (2007)
If a Tree Falls at Lunch Period by Gennifer Choldenko (2009)
The Penderwicks at Point Mouette by Jeanne Birdsall (2012)
The Reinvention of Moxie Roosevelt by Elizabeth Cody Kimmel (2011)
Summer of the Gypsy Moths by Sara Pennypacker (2013)
Throwing Heat by Fred Bowen (2010)
Waiting for Normal by Leslie Connor (2010)
Walk Two Moons by Sharon Creech (2011)
Weedflower by Cynthia Kadohata (2009)
Wild Life by Cynthia DeFelice (2011)
Wonderstruck by Brian Selznick (2011)

HISTORICAL FICTION

The Boy in the Stripped Pajamas by John Boyne (2007)
Boys of Wartime: Will at the Battle of Gettysburg by Laurie Calkhoven (2012)
The Bronze Bow by Elizabeth George Speare (1997)
Bud, Not Buddy by Paul Curtis (2004)
The Door in the Wall by Marguerite D'Angeli (1998)
The Dreamer by Pam Munoz Ryan (2012)
The Evolution of Calpurnia Tate by Jacqueline Kelly (2011)
A Faraway Island by Annika Thor (2009)
Forgotten Fire by Adam Bagdasarian (2002)
The Golden Goblet by Eloise Jarvis McGraw (1986)
Hatchet by Gary Paulsen (2006)
Lincoln's Last Days by Bill O'Reilly (2012)
Miss Spitfire: Reaching Helen Keller by Sarah Miller (2010)
My Last Skirt: The Story of Jennie Hodgers by Lynda Durrant (2006)
Revolution Is Not a Dinner Party by Ying Chang Compestine (2009)
Selling Hope by Kristin O'Donnell Tubb (2010)
Soldier Boys by Dean Hughes (2003)
The Stage Is Coming! Hallie's Stage Stop Journey by Rosalie Vandewater Ingle (2011)
A Thousand Never Evers by Shana Burg (2009)
Tropical Secrets: Holocaust Refugees in Cuba by Margarita Engle (2009)
The Trouble with May Amelia by Jennifer L. Holm (2012)
The True Confessions of Charlotte Doyle by Avi (2012)

MYSTERY AND SUSPENSE

Chomp by Carl Hiaasen (2013)
The Haunting by Joan Lowery Nixon (2000)
The Last Dog on Earth by Daniel Ehrenhaft (2004)
The London Eye Mystery by Siobhan Dowd (2009)
The Seer of Shadows by Avi (2009)
Tentacles by Rowland Smith (2011)
The Thief of Always by Clive Barker (2008)

FANTASY AND SCIENCE FICTION

Dragon Slippers by Jessica Day George (2008)
The Emerald Atlas by John Stephens (2012)
Eragon by Christopher Paolini (2005)
Gregor, The Overlander by Suzanne Collins (2004)
The Last Musketeer by Stuart Gibbs (2012)

The Limit by Kristen Landon (2011)
The Lion, the Witch and the Wardrobe by C. S. Lewis (2000)
The Magic Thief by Sarah Prineas (2009)
The Museum of Thieves by Lian Tanner (2011)
The Outcasts: Brotherband Chronicles by John Flanagan (2012)
Rise of the Darklings by Paul Crilley (2011)
The Silver Bowl by Diane Stanley (2012)
The True Meaning of Smekday by Adam Res (2009)
A Wrinkle in Time: The Graphic Novel by Madeleine L'Engle (2012)

POETRY

Classic Poems for Girls (audio CD) by Lewis Carroll, Edward Lear, Robert Louis Stevenson, and Christina Rosetti (2012)
Edgar Allan Poe's Stories and Tales (cassette) by Edgar Allan Poe and full cast (2000)
In Their Own Voices: A Century of Recorded Poetry (audio CD) by Erica Jong, Al Young, and Rebekah Presson (1997)
Poetry for Young People: Edgar Allan Poe by Brod Bagert (2008)
Poetry for Young People: Emily Dickinson by Frances Schoonmaker Bolin (2008)
Poetry for Young People: Henry Wadsworth Longfellow by Frances Schoonmaker Bolin (2008)
Poetry for Young People: Langston Hughes by David Roessel (2013)
Poetry for Young People: Lewis Carroll by Edward Mendelson (2008)
Poetry for Young People: Maya Angelou edited by Dr. Edwin Graves Wilson (2013)
Poetry for Young People: Robert Frost by Gary Schmidt (2008)
Poetry for Young People: Robert Louis Stevenson by Frances Schoonmaker Bolin (2008)
Poetry for Young People: William Shakespeare edited by David Scott Kastan (2008)
The Children's Homer (audio CD) by Padraic Colum and Robert Whitfield (2000)

SUGGESTED ACTIVITIES

- Compare and Contrast—In-class discussions on how to cite a source, create an example of APA, Chicago, and MLA or other formats your teacher wants you to use. Select a one-author text, a magazine article, and an online reference source. Your teacher may give you other suggestions. Discuss how each is similar and different. Keep the examples for future reference. (RL.6.1)

- Take Notes—Create a variation of the two-column notes when citing evidence. On the left side of your notes, label the column Explicit Details/Examples, and on the right side, label the column Inferred Details/Examples. As you take notes, write your responses in the appropriate column and include page numbers for future discussion. (RL.6.1)
- Cooperative Learning—In small groups, play interactive online games to learn how to create citations in APA or MLA. Go to http://depts.washington.edu/trio/quest/citation/apa_mla_citation_game/indes.htm. (RL.6.1)
- Nonlinguistic Representations—Create posters, dioramas, collages, or murals to illustrate specific and inferred details in the text, adding the page numbers to the illustrations. Be prepared to share your evidence in small group or class discussion. (RL.6.1, SL.6.1)
- Questions—Use stem questions in appendix C to help students cite textual evidence. (RL.6.1)
  - Use questions such as "What might you infer from . . . ?" or "Explain which clues or details from the text helped you to infer . . . "
- Make Predictions—Look at the title of your selection. Based solely on the title, make a prediction about what will happen in the story. As you get to the middle of the selection, make additional predictions. Cite page numbers to support your thinking. Continue to the end and check your predictions. Be ready to state the personal experience that led you to your predictions. Was your prediction correct? What are the similarities and differences in what you experienced and what happened in the text? (RL.6.1, SL.6.1)
- Hypothesize and Test—Cite textual evidence to support analysis when working to generate and test hypotheses. (RL.6.1)
- Questions—When you think about citing a source, what questions do you need to answer? (RL.6.1)
  - What format am I to use?
  - What information from the text do I need?
  - Where is a good place to look on the Internet if I have a question on a citation?
- Homework and Practice—Use various games and activities from the book *Plagiarism! Plagiarism! 25 Fun Games and Activities to Teach Documenting and Sourcing Skills to Students* by Kathleen Fox (2010). (RL.6.1)
- Homework and Practice—Practice citations by going on a citation hunt. Go to the website http://www.education.com/activity/article/Citation_Hunt_middle. (RL.6.1)

Strategies and Activities for Reading Literature 31

- Homework and Practice—Search texts for information and cite references in appropriate formats, http://www.brighthubeducation.com/middle-school-english-lessons/11380-scavenger-hunt-to-learn-about-referencing-and-citations. (RL.6.1)
- Compare and Contrast—Compare and contrast the treatment of theme in stories or poems. Create a graphic organizer such as a Venn diagram or T-chart. Select three stories or poems with the same themes and show the similarities and differences in how the theme is conveyed through details. You may share your organizer in group or class discussion. (RL.6.2, SL.6.1)
- Compare and Contrast—Select two or three stories from the exemplars or other grade-appropriate selections and create a two- or three-circle Venn diagram to compare and contrast the settings, events, and themes in the texts. You may share your diagrams with the group or class. (RL.6.2, SL.6.1)
- Summarize—Write a brief summary for each resource you are going to use in research, including the citation for the source. Add page numbers as you use the resource. The summary will help you as you write to remember the information from each source. (RL.6.2, RL.6.1)
- Summarize—Refer to the organizational chart created for fiction. Select two texts with similar themes or central ideas. Complete a narrative frame to summarize each text. Create a T-chart to compare and contrast the two texts. (RL.6.2)
- Summarize—Use the title of the book or story or poem and create an acrostic summary. (RL.6.2, W.6.10)
- Summarize—Do a quick write—a thirty to sixty second draft—to summarize what you have learned or have done with regard to a topic. (RL.6.2)
- Summarize—Complete a SQRRR (Survey/Question/Read/Recite/Review) summary frame on your current reading assignment. (RL.6.2, RL.6.3, RL.6.4, RL.6.5, RL.6.10)
- Summarize—Create a plot diagram to summarize a text or to show how the plot unfolds in a series of episodes or how the characters respond to situations. (RL.6.2, RL.6.3)
- Summarize—Use the Somebody-Wanted-But-So-Then summary frame to summarize the text. (RL.6.2)
- Summarize—Create a rap or song based on your notes and summaries of events. (RL.6.2)
  - Create mnemonics to help remember key details of people or events.
- Take Notes—Create a journal or a spreadsheet (paper or electronic) for fiction to identify the title, author, theme or central idea of the text, points of view, setting, characters, and key character behav-

iors. Highlight inferred details. Indicate page numbers that help you determine the information. (RL.6.2, RL.6.1)
- Nonlinguistic Representation—Create a comic strip to illustrate the theme of or to summarize a selection. (RL.6.2)
- Nonlinguistic Representation—Role play or pantomime key scenes to convey the theme or central idea of a selection. (RL.6.2, SL.6.6)
- Nonlinguistic Representation—Create concept webs or illustrated timelines to summarize selections. (RL.6.2)
- Nonlinguistic Representation—Select a graphic novel from the list or other appropriate selection and create an illustrated book jacket to summarize the text. (RL.6.2)
- Nonlinguistic Representation—Create book jackets or book marks for stories, poems, and drama to illustrate the theme. The illustrations or drawings should be representative of particular details. (RL.6.2)
- Cooperative Learning—As you read, conduct a Kagan Cooperative Learning[1] structure called Paraphrase Passport to summarize a larger selection. Students collaborate in groups of four. The first student begins to summarize the story or selection. The next student must paraphrase what the first student said and then contribute more to the summary. The process continues until all have had a chance to listen and to speak. Groups should alternate positions so the same student is not always first or last. (RL.6.2, SL.6.1)
- Cooperative Learning—Use the Kagan Cooperative Learning[2] structure of Think-Pair-Share. After reading a selection, get into pairs and think about the theme or central idea. You may also write out your thoughts as you think about the theme or central idea. One partner then shares their theme, citing textual evidence, while the other partner listens; then partners switch roles and repeat the process. (RL.6.2, SL.6.1)
  - Use Think-Pair-Share to share the day's reading or library book assignment.
- Predictions—Write words on file cards or small note cards that are relevant to the story you are discussing in class. You will need fifteen words for each pair of students; students are to place cards on their desk with words down. Ask students to create a T-chart on paper, labeling the left side "Words" and the right side "Predictions." Students then turn over five cards and write the words on the left side of their chart. Pairs silently think about the words for one minute in terms of theme or central idea. Pairs converse and make a prediction based on the words, writing the prediction on the right side of the paper. Repeat the process two more times, until all words have been revealed and three predictions have been made. Predictions may be changed as the new words appear. Let

students share their predictions with the class. Read the selection to determine the theme or central idea. (RL.6.2, SL.6.1)
- Questions—Use stem questions from appendix C to help determine the theme or central idea of a text and how it is conveyed. (RL.6.2)
- Homework and Practice—Write a paragraph to describe how the theme or central idea is conveyed in a story, citing page numbers to support your analysis. Which details helped you determine the theme or central idea? You may share your ideas in group or class discussion. (RL.6.2, RL.6.1, W.6.10)
- Homework and Practice—Practice writing summaries for various texts. (RL.6.2, W.6.10)
- Homework and Practice—Before reading a graphic novel, look at the illustrations. Can you infer the theme? Cite textual evidence to support your analysis. Then read the text to check your inferences. (RL.6.2, RL.6.1)

    Amelia Rules! by Jimmy Gownley (2009)
    The Arrival by Shaun Tan (2007)
    Artemus Fowl: The Graphic Novel by Eoin Colfer (2007)
    Beowulf by Gareth Hinds (2007)
    Bone: The Complete Cartoon Epic in One Volume (graphic novel) by Jeff Smith (2004)
    Captain Underpants (collection) by Dav Pilkey (2002)
    Coraline: The Graphic Novel by Neil Gaimann (2009)
    The Diary of a Wimpy Kid (series) by Jeff Kinney (2011)
    The Girl Who Owned a City by Dan Jolley (2012)
    The Graveyard Book by Neil Gaiman (2010)
    The Invention of Hugo Cabret by Brian Selznick (2007)
    The Lightning Thief: The Graphic Novel by Rick Riordan (2010)
    Maus: A Survivor's Tale by Art Spiegelman (2003)
    The Odyssey by Gareth Hinds (2010)
    The Red Pyramid by Rick Riordan (2012)
    Sign of the Black Rock by Scott Chantler (2011)
    Stormbreaker: The Graphic Novel by Antony Johnston (2006)
    Tales from Outer Suburbia by Shaun Tan (2009)
    Usagi Yojimbo (series) by Stan Sakai (2013)

- Compare and Contrast—Create a graphic organizer (concept web, double-T chart, etc.) to detail how the setting was used in the story considering the components of time, place, and the social environment of the characters (customs, dress, social manners, etc.) As you read, cite evidence to support your analysis. Do the setting details simply describe where the action takes place, or does where it take place affect the events? Use your notes to write an essay to compare and contrast the role of settings in two similar stories you select.

Edit your essay for grammar and mechanics. (RL.6.3, RL.6.1, W.6.2, L.6.1, L.6.2)
- Compare and Contrast—Create and complete problem-solution frames for stories or poems as you read. Compare selections with similar problems and contrast the solutions using a T-chart or Venn diagram to show how characters responded or changed. Jot down page numbers to cite your evidence in support of your analysis. (RL.6.3, RL.6.1)
- Compare and Contrast—Create a multicolumn chart to describe multiple characters in the same text (no more than five). You will need a column for each character and a row for each of the following: physical description, what the character says, what others say about the character, what the character does. Make note of the page numbers beside each detail or inference. Use the information to write a comparison and contrast essay to show how they are like the character, how they are different, and how their characteristics affect the plot. Edit your writing for grammar and mechanics. (RL.6.3, RL.6.1, W.6.2, L.6.1, L.6.2)
- Take Notes—Create a plot diagram for your story or selection. Jot down page numbers on the diagram to indicate the location of the details for quick reference. Also, highlight inferred information and be ready to support your information in group or class discussion. Use the Freytag form for your diagram that includes the exposition, rising action, climax, falling action, and resolution. Be prepared to share your diagram in group discussion. (RL.6.3, RL.6.1, SL.6.1)
- Take Notes—Use a narrative, problem-solution, Somebody-Wanted-But-So-Then frame, plot diagram, or timeline to show how the plot unfolds in a series of episodes as you read. (RL.6.3)
- Nonlinguistic Representation—As you read, document on a double timeline events and responses. Draw a line on your paper. On the top of the line, draw a picture to illustrate an event. Directly under the event, draw another picture to illustrate how the character responded or changed. Continue to end of story or selection. (RL.6.3)
- Nonlinguistic Representation—Create a concept web of important details in a story, poem, or drama to illustrate the relationship between the plot, setting, and characters. (RL.6.3)
- Nonlinguistic Representation—Role-play or read aloud the key episodes in a story, drama, or poem. Include visuals where needed to clarify meaning. (RL.6.3, SL.6.5, SL.6.6)
- Nonlinguistic Representation—Write and present a skit based on the key episodes and character responses in a story or drama. (RL.6.3, W.6.3, SL.6.5, SL.6.6)
- Cooperative Learning—Listen to several radio shows that can be downloaded free at www.oldtimeradiofans.com. Working in a small group, rewrite a story or drama into separate episodes that

would be similar to ones on the old time radio website. Record your stories adding music and sound where appropriate and share them with your classmates or other grade levels. (RL.6.3, W.6.3, SL.6.1, SL.6.5, SL.6.6)

- Hypothesize and Discuss—Think about the setting of a story. As a group or a class, work together to answer this question: How is the setting significant to character development or plot resolution? Create an if/then statement and discuss. For example, *if* the setting of a story is significant to the story, *then* the setting is significant in character development. Or, *if* the setting of a story is significant to the story, *then* the setting is significant to the plot resolution. (RL.6.3, SL.6.1)
- Hypothesize and Test—What happens if the setting is changed in a realistic fiction text? Can the events still happen? Why or why not? Rewrite a story or tell a story, changing key details of the setting to test your hypothesis. (RL.6.3, W.6.3)
- Hypothesize and Test—What happens if the setting is changed in a historical fiction text? Can the events still happen? Why or why not? Rewrite a story or tell a story, changing key details of the setting to test your hypothesis. (RL.6.3, W.6.3)
- Hypothesize and Test—If a historical event is changed, how are the characters affected? Rewrite a story or tell a story, changing key details of the event to test your hypothesis. (RL.6.3, W.6.3)
- Homework and Practice—Choose three different characters you have read about from the same selection. Create a three-circle Venn diagram to illustrate the similar and different character traits of all three characters. Note the page numbers of your evidence or inferences. Based on the information in your diagram, write an essay to show how each character responded or changed as the plot moved forward and attribute the response or change to one or more character traits. Edit your essay for grammar and mechanics. (RL.6.3, RL.6.1, W.6.2, L.6.1, L.6.2)
- Homework and Practice—Create a timeline for three main characters to illustrate how or if they changed from the beginning of the story to the end of the story. Make a concluding statement about which character changed the most and the least. Share with a partner or group or class. (RL.6.3, SL.6.1)
- Homework and Practice—Write a news story headline to show how the main character responded or changed as the plot moved forward. (RL.6.3, W.6.10)
- Compare and Contrast—Choose two fictional texts on similar topics, one that is rich with figurative language and/or connotative meanings and another that contains neither. Write an essay to compare and contrast the two selections. Cite specific evidence to sup-

port your analysis. Which is the more appealing of the two selections? (RL.6.4, RL.6.1, W.6.2)
- Take Notes—Create a class word wall and add and sort words as you learn them. (RL.6.4)
- Take Notes—Create a card file with index cards. As you come to a new word, write the word on a card, along with the definition as it is used in the sentence; note any affixes and their meanings as well as the word derivation. Also note whether the word is an example of regional or historical dialect. (RL.6.4)
  - Sort words throughout the year by affixes, roots, or derivations.
  - Add definitions to words or phrases as they are used in different context.
  - Add figurative language words and phrases as you see them in text.
- Take Notes—Take notes on how writers convey meaning in a text and analyze their word choices. (RL.6.4)
  - Read selections from the following or other appropriate sources:

    A Chocolate Mousse for Dinner by Fred Gwynne (1988)
    Dear Deer: A Book of Homophones by Gene Barretta (2010)
    The King Who Rained by Fred Gwynne (1988)
    A Little Pigeon Toad by Fred Gwynne (1988)

- In small group or class discussion, describe how the author's use of selected words adds to the humor of the text. Why does the author use homophones? Jot down page numbers to cite textual evidence to support your analysis. (RL.6.4, SL.6.1)
- Take Notes—Create a class dictionary. As you learn new words throughout the year, ask a volunteer to write the new word in the class dictionary. Use a three-ring binder with loose-leaf paper and alphabetical tabs so you can add to it throughout the year. Define the word or phrase as it is used in context. You may also create an electronic form of it as well using Word or another program. Students may look up the words or phrases as needed. Include poetry terms and definitions as well. (RL.6.4)
- Take Notes—Use an Alphabox to organize and define new words and phrases for each new story, poem, or unit. You may wish to create an electronic form in Excel so the size of the boxes can easily be adjusted to fit terms and definitions. (RL.6.4)
- Cooperative Learning—Get into pairs. Each of you will select five words from your word wall, card file, or maybe a dictionary. Write the words down. Do a Kagan Cooperative Learning[3] structure

called Think-Pair-Share as you both think about your words and how they make you feel. Then one at a time, share your words, their definitions, and the connotative meaning. (RL.6.4, SL.6.1)
- Questions—Use stem questions to ask about meanings of unknown words and phrases (RL.6.4)
    - What is the meaning of . . . ?
    - Using context clues, how would you define . . . ?
    - What clues helped you to define the word or phrase . . . ?
- Homework and Practice—Practice reviewing word meanings and connotations using crossword puzzles. Create your own crossword puzzles and share with the class. There are several puzzle makers on the Internet or you can use graph paper and create your own. (RL.6.4)

    http://www.puzzle-maker.com
    http://www.discoveryeducation.com/free-puzzlemake
    http://edhelper.com/crossword_free.htm
    http://worksheets.theteacherscorner.net/make-your-own/crossword

- Homework and Practice—Practice defining words using a definition frame and print or digital resources. (RL.6.4, SL.6.1)
    - Create flashcards with terms and definitions; work in pairs to quiz each other.
- Homework and Practice—In William Shakespeare's play *Romeo and Juliet*, Juliet says, "What's in a name? that which we call a rose / By any other name would smell as sweet . . ." Discuss the following questions in class: What is the connotation of rose in the sentence? What if Shakespeare had chosen the word ragweed? Would the connotation be the same? Choose a favorite line in a story, drama, or poem and write it down on paper. Analyze the impact of one specific word or phrase in your sentence. The word or phrase could be a metaphor, simile, hyperbole, or a repeated word. Share your sentence and word or phrase with the group or class and describe the impact it has on the meaning and tone. (RL.6.4, SL.6.1)
- Homework and Practice—Choose a poem the class is going to read. Enlarge the copy so you can cut up individual lines, giving one line to each student. Ask students to think about their line as to the meaning of the words, including figurative and connotative meanings. Ask students to read their line, give meaning to unknown words or phrases, and state the word or phrase that impacts the meaning or tone of the line and how. (RL.6.4, SL.6.1)
- Homework and Practice—Identify examples of figurative and descriptive language in various texts. Share examples with the class in

class discussion and discuss how figurative and descriptive language add to the overall quality of the text. (RL.6.4, SL.6.1)
- Take Notes—As you read, create a chart to identify how mood and plot are established in a story, poem or drama. The chart should indicate the sentence, chapter, scene, and/or stanza with the page number for quick reference, and should indicate whether mood or plot is established with the example. (RL.6.5, RL.6.1)
- Take Notes—As you read, identify and cite examples of personification and exaggeration. Describe what is being personified and how and/or what is exaggerated. Describe how each contributes to the plot development. (RL.6.5)
- Take Notes—Create T-charts to identify specific examples of personification as you read; cite the example, including page numbers, on one side and state how it is personification on the other side of the chart. You may be asked to share your responses with your group or class. (RL.6.5, SL.6.1)
- Nonlinguistic Representation—Role-play or read aloud the sentence, chapter, scene, or stanza that contributes to the development of the theme, setting, or plot. How does that selection fit the overall structure of the text? Cite specific details to support your thoughts. (RL.6.5, RL.6.1, SL.6.1, SL.6.6)
- Homework and Practice—Practice selecting a passage, stanza, or scene and journaling about how it fits into the overall structure of a text and contributes to the development of the theme, setting or plot. Share your thoughts with a partner. At the end of the selection, do you still think your passage was critical to the structure, theme, setting or plot? Why or why not? Cite specific details from the text. (RL.6.5, RL.6.1, SL.6.1)
- Homework and Practice—Create a class chart to reflect the forms of various plot structures such as chronological, fractured, framed, or circular. Your chart should describe each form and include examples of each that may be found as you read throughout the year. (RL.6.5)
- Homework and Practice—Create a class concept web or other appropriate graphic organizer to define the purposes and characteristics of satire, parody, and monologue. As you read, add examples (titles) of each to the chart. Choose a sentence from one of the examples listed (or other appropriate titles) and describe to a partner or in class discussions how it fits into the overall structure of the text and how it contributes to the development of the theme, setting, or plot. (RL.6.5, RL.6.1, W.6.3, SL.6.1, SL.6.5, SL.6.6)
    - Satire—
        - Compare and contrast the original version of *The Three Little Pigs* by Patricia Siebert (2002) to the Jon Scieszka

and Lane Smith book *The True Story of the Three Little Pigs* (1996) using a Venn diagram. Identify a specific sentence that lets you identify the story as satire. Read the sentence to the group or class and explain how it fits into the story as an example of satire.
- Other satirical examples include *The Butter Battle Book* by Dr. Seuss (1984) and *The Sneetches and Other Stories* by Dr. Seuss (1961). Identify which sentences, chapters, or scenes fit into the structure of the text and contributes to the development of the theme, setting, or plot.
- As you read, identify specific sentences, chapters, scenes, or stanzas that illustrate the author's use of mood, imagery, exaggeration, plot structure, or personification; cite textual evidence to support your analysis of what the text says explicitly or is inferred in group or class discussions. Describe how the use of these literary elements contribute to the development of the plot, theme, or setting.

- Parodies—
  - Compare and contrast an original poem to its parody using a Venn diagram, T-chart or other appropriate graphic organizer. Describe what changed and how and discuss how the meaning changed. Examples include:

    "I Must Go Down to the Sea Again" by John Masefield to "I Must Go Down to the Beach Again and Other Poems" by Karen Jo Shapiro (2007)

    Goodnight, Moon by Margaret Wise Brown (2007) to *Goodnight, iPad: A Parody for the Next Generation* by Ann Droyd (2011)

    "The Night before Christmas" by Clement Clarke Moore to "The Tale of St. Picklas" by Nicholas Pfeiffer (2011)

  - Check out the site bussongs.com or parody-song.php for other examples of parodies for kids.
  - As you read, identify specific sentences, chapters, scenes, or stanzas that illustrate the author's use of mood, imagery, exaggeration, plot structure, or personification; cite from the text to support your evidence or inferences in group or class discussions. Describe how the use of these literary elements contributes to the development of the plot, theme, or setting.

- Monologue—
    - Write a monologue based on a historical fiction character or a biography you have read; present the monologue to the class.
    - Role-play your monologue using multimedia components and visual displays to clarify information.
    - Create a bio-poem of a real or imagined character and present it as a monologue.
    - Make selections from *Finally, Monologues That Work (Ages 4–18)* by Christine Kolenik (2006) and present them to the class.
    - As you read, identify specific sentences, chapters, scenes, or stanzas that illustrate the author's use of mood, imagery, exaggeration, plot structure, or personification; cite from the text to support your evidence or inferences in group or class discussions. Describe how the use of these literary elements contribute to the development of the plot, theme, or setting.
- Homework and Practice—Write a critique about the text as a whole, evaluating how well the text, illustrations, and other features work together to develop the theme, setting or plot. Describe how each part individually works to develop the theme, setting, or plot. Edit your writing for grammar and mechanics. (RL.6.5, W.6.2, L.6.1, L.6.2, L.6.3)
- Homework and Practice—Analyze the use of flashback, the linking of current events to previous events, by authors. State the flashback and explain the relevance of the flashback. (RL.6.5)
    - Use such texts as

        "The Road Not Taken" by Robert Frost
        "Birches" by Robert Frost
        "The Odyssey" by Homer
        "The Midnight Ride of Paul Revere" by Henry Wadsworth Longfellow
        "Spring Rain" by Sara Teasdale
        "The Tell-tale Heart and Other Stories" by Edgar Allan Poe
        One Small Bead by Byrd Baylor (1992)
        Miss Rumphius by Barbara Cooney (1985)
        In My Own Backyard by Judi Jurjian (2000)
        Pink and Say by Patricia Polacco (1994)
        Why the Chicken Crossed the Road by David Macaulay (1987)
        House on Maple Street by Bonnie Pryor (1992)
        Wreck of the Zephyr by Chris Van Allsburg

- Take Notes—Analyze how particular sentences, chapters, scenes, or stanzas fit into the structure of various plot formats of fractured fairy tales, framed stories (story within a story), and circular stories. Create a T-chart that identifies the sentence, chapter, scene, or stanza on one side and describes how it fits the structure on the other side. You may share your responses in group or class discussion. (RL.6.5, SL.6.1)
    - Fractured Fairy Tales—Compare and contrast original fairy tales to fractured tales using a Venn diagram. You can use such stories as
        > *Cinderella Outgrows the Glass Slipper and Other Zany Fractured Fairy Tales* by Joan M. Wolf (2002)
        > *Fractured Fairy Tales for Student Actors: A Collection of Contemporary Fairy Tale Scenes* by Jan Peterson Ewen (2013)
        > *12 Fabulously Funny Fairy Tale Plays* by Justin McCory Martin (2002)
    - Framed Stories—In journal format, describe how stories within stories contribute to the development of the plot. Use such stories as
        > *The Canterbury Tales (Puffin Classics)* as retold by Geraldine McCaughrean (1997)
        > *Tales from the 1000 and One Nights (Penguin Classics)* by Anonymous
    - Circular Stories—create circle plot diagrams. Use texts such as
        > *Alice in Wonderland* by Lewis Carroll (1993)
        > *Anansi and the Moss-Covered Rock* by Eric Kimmell (1990)
        > *The Chronicles of Narnia* by C. S. Lewis (2001)
        > *If You Give a Mouse a Cookie* by Laura Numeroff (2010)
        > *Jack and the Beanstalk* (various authors)
        > *The Odyssey* by Homer
        > *The Relatives Came* by Cynthia Rylant (2009)
        > *The Wizard of Oz* by L. Frank Baum (various dates)
- Hypothesize and Test—What would happen if you took sentences, chapters, scenes, or stanzas from a story, drama, or poem? Does the text still make sense? Do the rest of the chapters, scenes, or stanzas fit together? Do the deletions affect the overall structure of the text? Is the development of the plot affected? Write a hypothesis and test it. If you took three chapters, scenes, or stanzas from text by the same author, would they fit together? (RL.6.5)

- Questions—Use stem questions in appendix C to ask about parts of stories, dramas, and poems and the structural elements in text. (RL.6.5)
  - What are the similarities and differences in the structural elements of . . . ?
  - How does the sentence, chapter, scene, or stanza fit into the overall structure of the text?
  - How well does _____ contribute to the theme, setting, or plot?
  - Describe the relationship between the sentence, chapter, scene, or stanza and the plot.
  - What might you infer from the sentence, chapter, scene, or stanza?
  - What was the most important sentence, chapter, scene, or stanza in the text and why?
- Homework and Practice—Write a position paper to support your analysis of how a particular sentence, chapter, scene, or stanza fits into the overall structure of a text and contributes to the development of the theme, setting, or plot. Edit your writing for grammar and mechanics. (RL.6.5, W.6.2, L.6.1, L.6.2, L.6.3)
- Compare and Contrast—Choose a selection from the Grades 6–8 text exemplars or other grade-appropriate texts. Create one character map for each of two characters from the same text by folding a piece of paper into four equal sections. Write the characters' names at the top of the page. In one square, state what other characters think about your character. In the rest of the squares, state how you feel about your character, what your character says and does, and how your character looks and what he feels. Repeat for the second character. Jot down page numbers in each square that helped you with the information for that square. Mark inferred information with a highlighter. Edit writing for grammar and mechanics. (RL.6.6, RL.6.1, W.6.2, W.6.10, SL.6.1, L.6.1, L.6.2, L.6.3)
  - Use the character maps for group or class discussion about what the text says explicitly or infers, or to explain how the author develops the narrator's or speaker's point of view.
  - Use the character maps to write a comparison and contrast essay that describes the points of view of two or more characters.
  - Change up your character maps from time to time to include the actions/reactions of others to the character, personality traits, strengths/weaknesses, and attitudes of the characters toward each other.
- Compare and Contrast—Create a three-circle Venn diagram or other appropriate graphic organizer and chart the points of view of the

Strategies and Activities for Reading Literature 43

main characters. Write an essay using the information to compare and contrast either multiple points of view in the same story or multiple points of view on the same topic from different stories. You may be asked to share your information in small or large group discussions. Edit your writing for grammar and mechanics. Cite textual evidence to support your analysis. (RL.6.6, RL.6.1, W.6.2, SL.6.1, L.6.1, L.6.2, L.6.3)

- Compare and Contrast—Who is the narrator or speaker? How does the perspective of the narrator or speaker differ from others in the story? Compare and contrast in essay format what the narrator knows and what others do or do not know. Edit your writing for grammar and mechanics. (RL.6.6, W.6.2, L.6.1, L.6.2, L.6.3)
- Compare and Contrast—Determine the point of view of three main characters. Create a three-circle Venn diagram to illustrate the similarities and differences in the points of view of the characters. (RL.6.6)
- Summarize—Summarize the point of view of the main character using a Somebody-Wanted-But-So-Then summary frame. (RL.6.6)
- Take Notes—Identify the narrator or speaker and one other character in your text. Illustrate how the author developed the point of view of both characters using a T-chart. Think about the actions, decisions, and descriptions of each to help you determine the points of view. Cite textual evidence to support your analysis. (RL.6.6, RL.6.1)
- Take Notes—Read *Black Beauty* by Anna Sewell (2003), *If a Tree Falls at Lunch Period* by Gennifer Choldenko (2009), *The Last Dog on Earth* by Daniel Ehrenhaft (2004), or *The Great Unexpected* by Sharon Creech (2013). How does the choice of first or third person contribute to the reader's enjoyment? (RL.6.6)
- Take Notes—As you read *Eleven* by Sandra Cisneros (EX) use a multicolumn T-chart to determine the points of view of the main character and two others. Use column headings such as Character, Say, Think, Do, Others Say, Others Think, and Others Do. Add information to your chart as you find it and cite the page number for easy reference in group discussion. When your chart is complete, write a sentence or two to explain each character's point of view. (RL.6.6, RL.6.1, SL.6.1)
- Take Notes—Create a multicolumn chart or concept web to illustrate narrator or speaker points of view. Use headings such as Characters, Physical Description, Say, Think, Do, What Others Say, and Think about Them. Complete the chart or web as you read. When you have finished the story and the chart or web, get with a partner or in small or large group discussions and use the information to explain the narrator or speaker points of view. (RL.6.6)

- Hypothesize and Test—It does/does not make a difference whether a story is told in first or third person. State and test your hypothesis. Rewrite a passage told in first person to third person or third person to first person. Does the story make sense? Is it more or less realistic? Is the reader affected by the change? (RL.6.6)
- Hypothesize and Test—What would happen if all stories were told from the same point of view (first or third person)? What happens if you change the point of view of a character, narrator/speaker—how do the events change? Write a hypothesis and test it by rewriting sections of text to reflect the change in person and explain how this influences events. Share your revisions with the group or class. (RL.6.6, W.6.3, SL.6.1)
- Predictions—Read or look at the title, chapter titles (if there are any), textual features, illustrations, and any blurbs about the author for a selection you are reading. Predict the narrator's or speaker's point of view prior to reading based on the titles, illustrations, and blurbs. (RL.6.6)
- Questions—Use stem questions to ask about the points of view of the narrator/speaker and the other characters. (RL.6.6)
    - Who is the narrator and how do you know?
    - What is the narrator's point of view?
    - How does the author develop the narrator's or speaker's point of view?
    - In what person is the story told and how do you know?
    - How does the choice of first or third person contribute to the reader's enjoyment?
    - Why does the author say _____ when he or she really means _____?
    - What are the other points of view presented in the story?
- Homework and Practice—Illustrate how the author developed the narrator's or speaker's point of view by presenting key sections of your text to the class. Let others try to determine the point of view based on your presentation of the events. (RL.6.6, SL.6.6)
- Compare and Contrast—Read a story, poem, or excerpt. Listen to the audio version. Listen again as you follow along with the text. Use sticky notes to indicate places that are different. Write an essay to compare and contrast the audio version to the written version, noting the differences and possible reasons for the changes. Edit your writing for grammar and mechanics. (RL.6.7, W.6.2, W.6.4, W.6.5, W.6.6, L.6.1, L.6.2, L.6.3)

    You could use: *The People Could Fly* by Virginia Hamilton (EX) and *The People Could Fly* by Audio Bookshelf (2005)

Black Ships before Troy: The Story of the Iliad by Rosemary Sutcliff (EX) and *Black Ships Before Troy: The Story of the Iliad* by Cover to Cover Cassettes (1998)

The Wanderings of Odysseus by Rosemary Sutcliff (2005) and *The Wanderings of Odysseus* by Cover to Cover Cassettes (1999)

Narrative of the Life of Frederick Douglass, An American Slave Written by Himself (EX) and *Narrative of the Life of Frederick Douglass, An American Slave* audio CD, Tantor Media (2009)

Harriet Tubman: Conductor on the Underground Railroad by Ann Petry (EX) and *Harriet Tubman: Conductor on the Underground Railroad*, Recorded Books, LLC (1999)

James and the Giant Peach by Roald Dahl (2007), *James and the Giant Peach* CD (2013)

Jabberwocky by Lewis Carroll (EX) and *Jabberwocky* Audible Audio Edition, PC Treasures, Inc. (2007)

A Child's Garden of Verses by Robert Louis Stevenson (2007) and *A Child's Garden of Verses* audio CD, Mission Audio (2011)

- If a live version is available in your area, attend the performance and include it in your comparison and contrast essay.
- Read *Dragon Wings* by Laurence Yep (EX) and take notes on one side of a T-chart about things you "see" and "hear." Then listen to *Dragon Wings* CD (Golden Mountain Chronicles) (2007) and note what you "see" and "hear" from the CD on the other side of the chart. Use the information from your chart to write an essay that compares and contrasts the experience of reading a story, drama, or poem to listening to or viewing an audio, video, or live version, contrasting what you see and hear. Edit your essay for grammar and mechanics. (RL.6.7, W.6.2, L.6.1, L.6.2, L.6.3)

- Compare and Contrast—Read a story, drama, or poem. Create a concept web to document what you "see" and "hear" as you read. Create another concept web to document what you "see" and "hear" while listening to of viewing an audio, video, or live version of the text you read. Use the information from both webs to compare and contrast in small or large groups what you read to what you perceive when listening or watching. (RL.6.7, SL.6.1, SL.6.2)
- Compare and Contrast—Compare and contrast plays, scripts, and narratives using a three-circle Venn diagram. (RL.6.7)
    - Use texts such as

        Fluency Practice Read-Aloud Plays Grades 5–6 by Kathleen M. Hollenbeck (2006)

10 American History Plays for the Classroom Grades 4–8 by Sarah Glasscock (1999)
James and the Giant Peach: A Play by Roald Dahl (2007)

- Compare and Contrast—Compare and contrast texts in different forms or genres to similar themes and topics in essay format. Consider the experiences of immigrants. What types of experiences did they share? What experiences were different? Cite textual evidence to support your analysis. Edit for grammar and mechanics. (RL.6.9, W.6.2, L.6.1, L.6.2, L.6.3)

    Choose texts such as: *Tropical Secrets: Holocaust Refugees in Cuba* by Margarita Engle (2009)
    A Faraway Island by Annika Thor (2009)
    My Last Skirt: The Story of Jennie Hodgers Union Soldier by Lynda Durrant (2006)

- Compare and Contrast—Compare and contrast nonfiction to realistic or historical fiction in essay format. Select one nonfiction selection, one realistic or historical fiction selection, and a poem or song. Compare and contrast the forms with regard to characters, specific events, and theme. Cite textual evidence to support your analysis. Edit for grammar and mechanics. (RL.6.9, W.6.2, L.6.1, L.6.2, L.6.3)

    Select texts such as: *A Night to Remember: The Classic Account of the Final Hours of the Titanic* by Walter Lord, audio CD, Audio GO (2012)
    The Night Lives On: The Untold Stories and Secrets behind the Sinking of the Unsinkable Ship-Titanic by Walter Lord (1998)
    A Night to Remember by Walter Lord (EX)
    Titanic: Voices from the Disaster by Deborah Hopkinson (2012)
    The Sinking of the Titanic, graphic novel by Matt Doeden (2005)
    The First and Final Voyage: The Sinking of the Titanic by Stephanie True Peters (2008)
    Titanic Poetry, Music and Stories by Ken Rossignol (2013)

- Compare and Contrast—Compare and contrast nonfiction to realistic fiction in essay format. Compare and contrast characters, specific events, and theme. Cite textual evidence to support your analysis. Edit for grammar and mechanics. (RL.6.9, W.6.2, L.6.1, L.6.2, L.6.3)

    Nonfiction: *MLK: Journey of a King* by Tonya Bolden (2007)
    Nonfiction: *Remember: The Journey to School Integration* by Toni Morrison (2004)
    Fiction: *The Watson's Go to Birmingham—1963* by Christopher Paul Curtis (1996)
    Fiction: *The Other Side* by Jacqueline Woodson (2001)

- Compare and Contrast—Compare and contrast different forms with regard to characters, events and settings in essay format. How does the setting in one form help you understand the setting in the other and which do you prefer? Cite textual evidence to support analysis and edit essay for grammar and mechanics. (RL.6.9, RL.6.1, W.6.2, L.6.1, L.6.2, L.6.3)

    Freedom Walkers: The Story of the Montgomery Bus Boycott by Russell Freedman (EX)
    Rosa Parks and the Montgomery Bus Boycott: A Graphic Novel by Connie Colwell Miller (2007)

- Compare and Contrast—Compare and contrast in essay format or other appropriate form a nonfiction work to a biographical fiction work. Consider the genre, organization, style, and form in your essay. Cite textual evidence to support analysis and edit essay for grammar and mechanics. (RL.6.9, RL.6.1, W.6.2, L.6.1, L.6.2, L.6.3)

    Compare texts such as *The Life and Times of Frederick Douglass* by Frederick Douglass (2003) to *Frederick Douglass: Abolitionist Hero* by George Stanley (2008)

- Compare and Contrast—Choose two favorite characters, one each from stories and poems or one each from historical novels and fantasy. Create a two-circle Venn diagram to show how the characters were alike and different with regard to events that happened to them, character traits, or how they responded to situations. Use the information to write a comparison and contrast essay. Edit your essay for grammar and mechanics. (RL.6.9, W.6.2, L.6.1, L.6.2, L.6.3)
- Compare and Contrast—Choose one or two characters from your favorite story, poem, realistic or historical fiction. Create a two- or three-circle Venn diagram to detail how you are alike and unlike the characters you chose. Use the information to write a comparison and contrast essay. Edit your essay for grammar and mechanics. (RL.6.9, W.6.2, L.6.1, L.6.2, L.6.3)
- Take Notes—As you read throughout the year, note on a class chart or spreadsheet the title and genre, main character, key traits, important actions, and significant circumstances attributed to the main character. (RL.6.9)

    - Compare and contrast characters within and across various genres on the same topic. Consider any special or significant circumstances that surround the character and major actions and character traits. Choose any three characters from varying genre and write an essay to compare and contrast the characters so that you can see the connections between them even though they appear in different texts. Edit your essay for grammar and mechanics. (RL.6.9, W.6.2, L.6.1, L.6.2, L.6.3)

- Take Notes—As you read myths, legends, or tall tales, add to a class spreadsheet or chart the following information: title, country of origin, main character, setting, problem, hero, solution, and unique characteristics. (RL.6.9)
  - Review your chart or spreadsheet and select one character. How are you like/unlike that character? What unique characteristic do you have? Write a comparison and contrast essay to answer the questions. Cite evidence from the myth, legend, or tall tale in your description of the character. Edit your essay for grammar and mechanics. (RL.6.9, W.6.2, L.6.1, L.6.2, L.6.3)
- Homework and Practice—Read and comprehend literature in the Grades 6–8 text complexity band proficiently. (RL.6.10, SL.6.1, SL.6.6)
  - Practice reading every night, self-correcting when you make mistakes.
  - Stop frequently when reading and restate in your own words what you have read.
  - As you read, make mental predictions about what will happen next and check to see if you were correct.
  - Record stories or poems for others to hear.
  - Create skits or plays based on literary text.
  - Play music in the background related to theme and topics.
  - Dress in costume as you read—keep it simple—wear hats, scarves, vests; something symbolic of the topic or theme.
  - Role-play the main character in stories, drama, or poems.
  - Memorize and present favorite passages or poems.

    Partner Poems for Building Fluency: Grades 4–6: Engaging Poems for Two Voices by Tim Rasinski, David Harrison, and Gay Fawcett (2009)

    Read and Understand Poetry, Grades 5–6+ by Linda Armstrong (2005)

    Read Aloud Passages and Strategies to Model Fluency: Grades 5–6 edited by Danielle Blood (2007)

- Homework and Practice—To help students better visualize characters, individuals, events, and settings, incorporate a variety of visuals and experiences (RL.6.10)
  - Attend plays in your area.

- Post calendar pictures, book jackets, magazine, or other printed pictures around the room that represent your current topics and refer to them when taking notes.
- Look for original prints you could borrow from libraries or parents.
- Create areas in the room representative of settings or events.
- Create artifact tables—find pictures or symbolic replicas of items that represent people, characters, or events.
- Eat a meal that would be symbolic of your theme or topic.
- Listen to music that represents your topic during free time or played softly in the background while taking notes.

- Homework and Practice—Read aloud or listen to various grade level text. (RL.6.10)

NOTES

1. Kagan, S., & Kagan, M. (1997). *Kagan Cooperative Learning Smart Card* (pp. 2–3). San Clemente, CA: Kagan Publishing.
2. Kagan, S., & Kagan, M. (1997) for further information.
3. Kagan, S., & Kagan, M. (1997) for further information.

FIVE
Grade 6 Strategies and Activities for Reading Informational Text

Choose informational text from Grades 6–8 text exemplars selections which are noted with an (EX). Other appropriate grade level selections include, but are not limited to, the following:

AUTOBIOGRAPHIES

The Autobiography of Willie O'Ree: Hockey's Black Pioneer by Willie O'Ree (2000)
Ballerina: My Story by Darci Kistler (1993)
Hope Solo: My Story by Hope Solo (2013)
Jeff Corwin: A Wild Life by Jeff Corwin (2009)
The Life of P. T. Barnum, Written by Himself by P. T. Barnum (2000)
Man on a Mission: The David Hilmers Story by David Hilmers (2013)
Soul Surfer: A True Story of Faith, Family, and Fighting to Get Back on the Board by Bethany Hamilton (2012)
We Are Witnesses: Five Diaries of Teenagers Who Died in the Holocaust by Jacob Boas (2009)

BIOGRAPHIES

Almost Astronauts: 13 Women Who Dared to Dream by Tanya Lee Stone (2009)
Bethany Hamilton: Follow Your Dreams! by Michael Sandler (2006)
Beverly Cleary by Cari Meister (2001)
The Condoleezza Rice Story by Antonia Felix (2002)
Escape: The Story of the Great Houdini by Sid Fleischman (2008)

The Great and Only Barnum: The Tremendous, Stupendous Life of Showman P. T. Barnum by Candace Fleming (2008)
How They Croaked: The Awful Ends of the Awfully Famous by Georgia Bragg (2012)
Rosa Parks: Courageous Citizen by Ruth Ashby (2008)
Sadako and the Thousand Paper Cranes by Eleanor Coerr (2004)
Traitor: The Case of Benedict Arnold by Jean Fritz (1997)
Who Was Neil Armstrong? by Roberta Edwards (2008)
Who Was Leonardo Da Vinci? by Roberta Edwards (2005)
Who Was Walt Disney? by Whitney Stewart (2009)
Who Was Amelia Earhart? by Kate Boehm Jerome (2002)
Who Was Albert Einstein? by Jess Brailler et al. (2002)
Who Is Bill Gates? by Patricia Brennan Demuth (2013)
Who Is Jane Goodall? by Roberta Edwards (2012)
Who Was Steve Jobs? by Pam Pollack (2012)

MEMOIRS

A Girl from Yamhill: A Memoir by Beverly Cleary (1996)
Condoleezza Rice: A Memoir of My Extraordinary, Ordinary Family and Me by Condoleezza Rice (2010)
Dear Mrs. Parks: A Dialogue with Today's Youth by Gregory Reed and Rosa Parks (1997)
My Own Two Feet: A Memoir by Beverly Cleary
No Higher Honor: A Memoir of My Years in Washington by Condoleezza Rice (2011)

GENERAL NONFICTION

A Strong Right Arm: The Story of Mamie "Peanut" Johnson by Michelle Green (2004)
Amazing but True Sports Stories by Phyllis Hollander (1986)
Black Eagles: African Americans in Aviation by James Haskins (1997)
Children of the Dustbowl: The True Story of the School at Weedpatch Camp by Jerry Stanley (1993)
G Is for Googol: A Math Alphabet Book by David Schwartz (1998)
Immigrant Kids by Janet Bode (1995)
Journey into the Deep: Discovering New Oceans by Rebecca L. Johnson (2010)
Space, Stars and the Beginning of Time: What the Hubble Telescope Saw by Elaine Scott (2011)
They Had a Dream: The Civil Rights Struggle by Jules Archer (1996)
The Wall: Growing Up behind the Iron Curtain by Peter Sis (1997)
The Word Snoop by Ursula Dubosarsky (2009)

SUGGESTED ACTIVITIES

- Cooperative Learning—In small groups play interactive online games to learn how to create citations in APA or MLA. Go to http://depts.washington.edu/trio/quest/citation/apa_mla_citation_game/indes.htm. (RI.6.1)
- Homework and Practice—Use various games and activities from the book *Plagiarism! Plagiarism! 25 Fun Games and Activities to Teach Documenting and Sourcing Skills to Students* by Kathleen Fox (2010). (RI.6.1)
- Homework and Practice—Practice citations by going on a citation hunt. Go to the website http://www.education.com/activity/article/Citation_Hunt_middle. (RI.6.1)
- Homework and Practice—Search texts for information and cite references in appropriate formats. http://www.brighthubeducation.com/middle-school-english-lessons/11380-scavenger-hunt-to-learn-about-referencing-and-citations. (RI.6.1)
- Summarize—Read selected passages to determine the central idea of a text and how it is conveyed through particular details; then write a summary of the text distinct from personal opinions or judgments. (RI.6.2)
    - You might use *Non-fiction Reading Practice, Grade 6* by Ellen Linnihan (2003)
- Summarize—Create acrostic summaries using the title of the text. Share summaries in small groups or with the class. (RI.6.2)
- Summarize—Create concept webs, Somebody-Wanted-But-So-Then frames, problem-solution frames, narrative frames, and bio-poems to summarize text. (RI.6.2)
- Take Notes—Use a two-column note format. As you read, jot down on the left side what you think the central idea of a text is and on the right, jot down textual evidence to support what the text says and infers in support of your analysis. (RI.6.2, RI.6.1)
- Take Notes—Create outlines to detail main ideas and specific details to help determine the central idea of a text. (RI.6.2)
- Take Notes—Read a variety of texts with content applicable to today's sixth grade student such as self-esteem, academic pressures, bullying or other antisocial behaviors, or disappointment and rejection. As you read, take notes on the key points. Then in your journal, write how you can apply the information to your life today. You may also be asked to participate in class discussions on the issues. (RI.6.2, W.6.2, SL.6.1, L.6.1, L.6.2, L.6.3)

    The Complete Idiot's Guide to Surviving Peer Pressure for Teens by Hilary Cherniss (2001)

The Drama Years: Real Girls Talk about Surviving Middle School . . . Bullies, Brands, Body Image and More by Haley Kilpatrick and Whitney Joiner (2012)

Help! I'm in Middle School . . . How Will I Survive? by Merry Gumm (2005)

Teen Ink: Our Voices, Our Visions by John and Stephanie Meyer (2000)

- Create a concept web for each text to illustrate the central idea of each and how it was conveyed through particular details.
- Create a two- or three-circle Venn diagram to compare and contrast the information in two or three books. Consider the use of illustrations, main ideas, and supporting details.
- Decide which book is most helpful in your opinion to boys or to girls in terms of information presented. Write a position paper to defend your opinion.
- Create a book jacket with a summary on the back for each book.

- Cooperative Learning—As you are reading to determine the central idea, stop frequently to do a Think-Pair-Share.[1] When given the signal, think about the information you have just read, jotting notes or drawing pictures or symbols to help you remember particular details. Then pair up and take turns sharing your thoughts and information. (RI.6.2)
- Predictions—Prior to reading, make predictions at the beginning of the text based on the title, illustrations, chapter titles, or other textual features about the central idea of the text. In the middle of the text, make predictions about the end of the text. Write your predictions in a journal and cite textual evidence to support your predictions. (RI.6.2, RI.6.1)
- Homework and Practice—Choose your favorite nonfiction text and evaluate how well the author used illustrations and print to convey the central idea. Make note of textual evidence to support your claim. Present your evaluation to the group or class. (RI.6.2, RI.6.1, SL.6.1)
- Take Notes—Create a timeline to show inferred thought processes or problems in decision making of subjects or characters. Cite textual evidence leading to your inferences. (RI.6.3)
- Take Notes—Create a class chart or spreadsheet to analyze how nonfiction writers write. Include the following headings on your chart or spreadsheet: title of work, author, text organization, narrative elements, literary devices, writer's craft examples, and textual features. Text organization includes the sequence of chapters, me-

moir or storytelling, step-by-step, topic/category, cause/effect, problem/solution, comparison/contrast, or description/list. Narrative elements include setting, characters, plot, conflict, climax, and resolution. Literary devices include humor, irony, suspense, and symbolism. Writer's craft includes dialogue, definitions, textual divisions, descriptive language, verb usage, and leads. Textual features includes captions, maps, illustrations or photographs, glossaries, graphics, index, labels, special prints (italics, bold, etc.), subtitles, and table of contents. As you read each day, discuss the various elements used by writers to understand how individuals, events, and ideas are introduced, illustrated and elaborated in text. (RI.6.3, SL.6.1)

- Choose two selections by the same author or illustrator. Use a T-chart to compare and contrast how illustrations or graphics were used to help convey meaning or create the mood. Share your chart with the group or class.
- Take Notes—Add new words or phrases and their meanings to your word wall or vocabulary card file or notebook as they are used in context. Add new meanings to existing words or phrases as well. Designate words or phrases using a symbol or color to reflect regional or historical dialects as well as languages other than English. (RI.6.4)
- Take Notes—Complete a definition frame for words that have special historical significance. (RI.6.4)
- Take Notes—To help solidify a new word or phrase, write the term or phrase on an index card. Draw a picture or symbol that represents the word or phrase. Write down one example of the word or phrase. Write a hint to help you remember (such as a mnemonic). Write a sentence using the word or phrase. Share your pictures, examples, and sentences with the class. (RI.6.4)
- Take Notes—Nonfiction text structure refers to how the writer organizes and develops ideas. The most important text structures are description or list, sequence or time order, compare and contrast, cause and effect, and problem/solution (http://comsewogue.org/webpages/drosenquist/reading_workshop.cfm?subpage=640939). As you read make note of the structure(s) used and describe how each contributed to the development of ideas. Be prepared to share your thoughts in class discussion. (RI.6.5, SL.6.1)
- Take Notes—How well does your favorite nonfiction book fit the genre of nonfiction? What qualities or characteristics are seen in the text? Your nonfiction book should be accurate, objective and unbiased; be organized appropriate to the content; and contain a useful index; contain illustrations and photographs with correct descriptive captions and photo credits. The author should also be

qualified to write on the subject or have completed enough research to have creditable knowledge of the subject (http://www.education.com/reference/article/characteristics-good-nonfiction). You also need to consider the author's purpose and attitude toward the subject. With this in mind, create a content web, poster, or chart to illustrate how well your nonfiction book fits the genre or nonfiction. Cite page numbers for specific details or inferences taken from the book. (RI.6.5, RI.6.1)

- Take Notes—Read *Black Ships before Troy: The Story of the Iliad* by Rosemary Sutcliff (EX). As you read, create and complete a concept web or other graphic organizer to describe the ancient Greek society. Jot down page numbers of specific and inferred details. In class discussion describe how particular sentences, paragraphs, and sections contribute to the development of ideas. (RI.6.5, SL.6.1)
- Nonlinguistic Representation—Create an illustrated bookmark that represents a sentence, paragraph, section, or chapter that contributes the most to the development of the central idea. Write the title, author, sentence/paragraph/section/chapter, and page number on one side and put your illustration on the other. Share with a partner or the class. (RI.6.5, SL.6.1)
- Predictions—Perform a SQ (a Survey-Question) on your reading assignments. Based on section titles, headings, subheadings, illustrations/photographs, make predictions about what you will read. Then complete the RRR (Read-Recite-Review) and track your predictions as you read. (RI.6.5)
- Hypothesize and Test—How would your comprehension of the material be affected if you had no title, headings, illustrations, or photographs? Write and test your hypothesis. (RI.6.5)
- Homework and Practice—Choose your favorite nonfiction text. Write a position paper about how well a writer uses text, illustration, and other textual features to convey ideas. How well do all of the elements fit together? Cite specific examples to support your analysis. Edit your paper for grammar and mechanics. (RI.6.5, W.6.2, L.6.1, L.6.2, L.6.3)
- Compare and Contrast—Read various articles from different sources about the same topic or idea. Write an essay to compare and contrast the points of view of the different authors. Cite textual evidence to support analysis of what the text says explicitly and what it infers. Edit your essay for grammar and mechanics. You may be asked to share your thoughts in class discussion. (RI.6.6, RI.6.1, SL.6.1, L.6.1, L.6.2, L.6.3)
  - Work with a partner to create a Venn diagram to illustrate the points of view from two authors on the same topic.

Strategies and Activities for Reading Informational Text 57

- Summarize—Summarize the author's point of view to illustrate the bias in a biography, noting specific examples of biased language. (RI.6.6, RI.6.1, W.6.2)
- Take Notes—As you read, make note of examples of bias, citing the specific language used that reveals the bias. Note page numbers of the examples. (RI.6.6)
- Take Notes—Create a graphic organizer to illustrate the specific points of view given and how the author conveys them in the text. Jot down page numbers to support your evidence. (RI.6.6)
- Hypothesize and Test—Why would an author of a biography use biased language in his/her biography? Write and test a hypothesis for a biography you have read to determine the bias and the reason for the bias citing specific and inferred textual evidence. (RI.6.6, RI.6.1, W.6.2)
- Homework and Practice—The teacher will create or purchase a flat world wall map and post it on a wall in the classroom. At the beginning of the year as you read informational literature, indicate the country where the stories or events take place. When several are marked, choose the country you most want to learn more about and create a multimedia presentation with travel brochure on that country. Conduct research with a partner and develop a PowerPoint presentation with words and visuals that would make others want to visit the country with you. Include charts, graphs, maps, diagrams, and/or illustrations in your presentation. Prepare to present your presentation to the class. So that classmates will have something to remember your presentation, prepare a trifold brochure with pertinent information and visuals. Follow the formats provided by your teacher. Cite all sources used and edit your PowerPoint and brochure for mechanics and grammar. (RI.6.6, RI.6.1, RI.6.10, W.6.2, W.6.4, W.6.5, W.6.6, W.6.7, W.6.8, W.6.10, SL.6.1, SL.6.6, L.6.1, L.6.2, L.6.3)
  - After presentations are given, students will comment on how the information presented contributed to the topic of future travel to that country. (SL.6.2)
- Take Notes—As you read, use a two-column note format to track the types of graphics you see (maps, charts, pictures, captions, diagrams, illustrations, etc.) and note the information you learned from the graphic. Indicate page numbers for future reference. (RI.6.7)
- Take Notes—As you read historical fiction or informational text, note details and descriptions of setting in a journal or a class chart or spreadsheet. Use the setting details from one text to help you comprehend events in other texts on the same topic. (RI.6.7)

- Cooperative Learning—After a class presentation, do a Paraphrase Passport.[2] Students should get into groups of four. The first student makes comments or observations about a topic (such as why they would or would not visit the country presented) while the others listen. The next student must paraphrase what the first student said before adding his own comments or observations. The process continues around the group until all have paraphrased and contributed. (RI.6.7, SL.6.1)
- Questions—After hearing and viewing each class presentation, write out what questions you still have about the information in the presentation and participate in a Q&A with the presenter. (RI.6.7, SL.6.1)
- Summarize—Write a summary to trace the arguments and claims supported by reasons and evidence in text or presentations. (RI.6.8, RI.6.1, W.6.2)
- Take Notes—Create a concept web or other type of graphic organizer to illustrate an argument or claim and the supportive reasons and evidence. (RI.6.8)
- Take Notes—As you read or listen to informational text, use a table to track facts and opinions. (RI.6.8)
- Take Notes—As you read or listen to informational text, jot down examples of writer's or speaker's bias or use of exaggeration. Cite textual evidence to support your analysis. (RI.6.8, RI.6.1)
- Cooperative Learning—With a partner, read several stories, excerpts or interviews about the same topic or event (e.g., the Holocaust, the Great Depression, sinking of the Titanic). Create a Venn diagram to detail information that was similar and different between the texts. Identify, trace, and evaluate the argument and evidence in one story, excerpt, or interview and decide if the claims are supported by the evidence. Discuss with your partner possible reasons as to why differences would exist. Jot down your thoughts and be prepared to share them with the class. (RI.6.8, SL.6.1, SL.6.4)
- Cooperative Learning—Work with a partner to evaluate and determine the authenticity and quality of a text as well as the author's qualifications and background knowledge. Create a graphic organizer that illustrates the claims and supportive evidence of an argument. Then conduct a short research project to answer the questions: is the author qualified to present the argument and is the text presented authentic? Use several sources to answer your questions. Each claim and piece of evidence presented by the author should be cited and supported using additional resources. Cite textual evidence from your sources to substantiate the author's claims and evidence with page numbers and titles of sources. Your teacher may give you specific ways to cite your information. (RI.6.8, RI.6.1, W.6.2, W.6.7, SL.6.1)

- Homework and Practice—Practice tracing and evaluating arguments and claims and distinguishing claims supported by reason and evidence from those that do not. Read a selection from a mini-mystery and complete an argumentation frame based on the "argument" and "claims" presented in the text. Create and complete a table that lists the supported claims and those not supported. Cite the page numbers of the specific text that supports the claims made in the text. Be prepared to present your evaluation to the group or class. (RI.6.8, RI.6.1, SL.6.1, SL.6.4)

    Crime and Puzzlement: 24 Solve-Them-Yourself Picture Mysteries by Lawrence Treat (2003)
    Crime Files: Four-Minute Forensic Mysteries: Body of Evidence by Jeremy Brown (2006)
    Five-Minute Mysteries by Ken Weber (2005)
    Two-Minute Mysteries by Donald Sobol (1991)

- Homework and Practice—Analyze arguments and distinguish claims supported by reason and evidence from claims that are not as presented by classmates. Listen to the arguments and claims and evidence as presented. On your printed copy, highlight important information such as the argument or claim (main idea) in one color and evidence (supporting details) in another color. Use different colors for counterclaims and supportive evidence if it is found in the speech. Create a T-chart that lists the supported claims on one side and the unsupported claims on the other. Indicate specific text that supports the claims. Use the information on the T-chart in group or class discussion. (RI.6.8, SL.6.1, SL.6.4)
- Compare and Contrast—Compare and contrast one author's presentation of events with that of another using biographies, autobiographies, and memoirs. Create a T-chart to illustrate examples of style, theme, organization, events, characters, and ideas presented. Cite textual evidence to support your analysis. Use the information from the charts, webs, or diagrams to write a comparison and contrast essay. (RI.6.9, RI.6.1, W.6.2, L.6.1, L.6.2, L.6.3)

    - Use concept webs or Venn diagrams to compare and contrast information presented.
    - Compare and contrast fictional characters with real people who have similar traits or actions.

- Compare and Contrast—Compare and contrast a memoir or autobiography to a biography by creating a life graph timeline for each text. On the top of the timeline illustrate and identify events that were positive and put negative events on the bottom of the time line, all in chronological order. In class discuss, compare and contrast the two graphs, noting events that are similar to both

graphs and those that are different. In your discussion, discuss possible reasons why the authors chose to include or exclude events. (RI.6.9, SL.6.1)
- Compare and Contrast—In an essay, compare and contrast historical fiction and informational text based on the same time period (slavery, westward expansion). How are the accounts similar and different? Why would the accounts vary? Create a Venn diagram to use in prewriting. Edit your essay for grammar and mechanics. (RI.6.9, W.6.2, L.6.1, L.6.2, L.6.3)
- Take Notes—Determine the five most important facts you learned about a topic that either you researched or was presented by another student or group. Order them from the most to least important and support your choices. (RI.6.9)
- Hypothesize and Test—Read and/or listen to various versions of the same topics. Offer hypotheses about an issue in the stories or informational literature and try to establish evidence to prove their hypotheses. (RI.6.9)

NOTES

1. Kagan, S., & Kagan, M. (1997). *Kagan Cooperative Learning Smart Card* (pp. 2–3). San Clemente, CA: Kagan Publishing.
2. See Kagan, S., & Kagan, M. (1997) for further information.

SIX

Grade 6 Strategies and Activities for Writing

Choose literary and informational text from Grades 6–8 text exemplars selections or other appropriate grade level selections. Grades 6–8 text exemplars are noted with an (EX).

- Homework and Practice—Write arguments using various formats provided by your teacher. The introduction should contain a hook, background information, and a thesis statement; the body is three paragraphs that contain the reason or argument and supportive evidence. You also have a section in the body with counter arguments and responses. The final section is a conclusion that restates your thesis, summarizes the important points, and calls for an action. (http://img.docstoccdn.com/thumb/orig/119603186.png) (W.6.1)
- Homework and Practice—Write arguments to support claims with clear reasons and relevant evidence. Create a T-chart or other appropriate graphic organizer to state the claim or argument and brainstorm a list of the pros and cons of your claim. Select the best three pros or cons and write your argument. Compare and contrast your argument with those of classmates on similar topics. Edit your writing for grammar and mechanics. (W.6.1, SL.6.1, L.6.1, L.6.2, L.6.3)
    - Choose topics or ideas such as
        - Places to go for fieldtrips and why
        - Why girls and boys should or should not play on the same teams

- Why your favorite author should or should not come to your school
- Why school lunch should be improved
- The best ways to defend against bullying
- Pros and cons of early morning classes
- Chocolate milk vs. white milk
- Cell phones at school
- Curfews
- The school day should/should not be extended to increase the number of subjects students should know
- Facebook is a positive/negative form of social media
- Allow or remove pop/soda vending machines in school buildings
- Ways to prevent cheating on tests
- Video games have a negative impact on students
- Schools should/should not implement random book bag or locker checks for weapons
- Schools should purchase laptops for all students
- The most important quality a person can have
- There is too much violence in film/music/television
- Schools should/should not require physical education for all students
- To have or not have school uniforms or dress codes
- Reading a story is better than listening to it (or the opposite)
- Bus drivers should be armed with tasers to subdue fighting students
- Teachers should be armed in classrooms
- All students should participate in one extracurricular activity
- "A smooth sea never made a skilled mariner." (English proverb)
- It is better to be hated for what you are than loved for something you are not.
- It takes courage to grow up and become who you really should be.
- Are the reasons for immigration the same now as 200 years ago?
- Present an argument to your parents to grant permission for something you want (attend a concert, school dance, etc.)
- To help brainstorm for ideas, post the topics on chart paper around the room and allow students to share their ideas or thoughts or details on the chart paper.

Students can use the information to help with their arguments and evidence.

- Take Notes—Use outlines or other graphic organizers to take notes on topics for arguments, informative/explanatory texts, narratives, or other short research projects. (W.6.1, W.6.2, W.6.3, W.6.7, W.6.10)
- Homework and Practice—Identify a sentence, paragraph, chapter, stanza, or scene from your favorite book. Write an argument to support your claim that the selection you chose fits the overall structure of the story or text and contributes to the development of the theme, setting, plot or ideas. Present your argument to the group or class. (W.6.1, RL.6.5, RI.6.5, SL.6.1, SL.6.4, L.6.1, L.6.2, L.6.3)
    - Classmates should be able to delineate the speaker's argument and claims while creating a chart to illustrate supported reasons and evidence from those that are not. (SL.6.3)
- Nonlinguistic Representations—As you read this year, keep track on a large wall map made in class of the countries, states, or cities you read about. Select a country, state, or city you want to know more about. Talk with a partner and ask, If you could go to this place, what three things would you want to know? Conduct research to determine information about the country and culture and to answer the questions. Create a travel brochure or poster to illustrate the answers to your questions. Write copy to go along with your brochure. Share your travel brochure with the class. (W.6.2, RI.6.1, SL.6.1, SL.6.2)
- Questions—What are three facts that you didn't know about the subject of a biography, autobiography, and memoir that you read? How do you know the "facts" are true? Locate credible and reliable information to support your premise that the information is true about your person. Write an essay to explain what you learned and how you know it to be true. (W.6.2, W.6.4, W.6.5, W.6.6, W.6.7, L.6.1, L.6.2, L.6.3)
- Questions—Research the relationship between authors' lives and what they write about. Write an essay to answer this question: Why do you think the author writes about ____? Cite textual evidence to support your analysis of what the text says and infers. Check biographies, autobiographies, memoirs, letters, or interviews. Edit your writing for grammar and mechanics. (W.6.2, W.6.4, W.6.5, W.6.7, L.6.1, L.6.2, L.6.3)
- Homework and Practice—Read a biography of a favorite person and write a book review critiquing the presentation of the subject. Make note of any examples of bias. Present your critique to the class in the form of a five-paragraph essay. Follow the format pre-

sented by your teacher or use the following: a statement of what you are reviewing, three statements that support your opinion textually supported, and a final paragraph to restate your opinion and summarize your three points. Edit for grammar and mechanics. (W.6.2, RI.6.1, RI.6.6, SL.6.1, L.6.1, L.6.2, L.6.3)

- Classmates should be able to delineate the speaker's argument and claims while creating a chart to illustrate supported reasons and evidence from those that are not. (SL.6.3)
- You could also write a review of your favorite CD or movie; other reviews could include a favorite electrical device such as a computer, laptop, smart phone, etc. Consult *Consumer Reports* and interview friends and family members.

- Homework and Practice—Create a list of the three most important facts you learned from a presentation or a class topic and order the facts from most important to least important. Write a position paper about what you learned and why each fact was important. Edit your writing for grammar and mechanics. Your teacher may have a specific format for you to use. (W.6.2, RI.6.1, L.6.1, L.6.2, L.6.3)
- Homework and Practice—Write informative texts on a variety of topics. Cite textual evidence when appropriate. Your teacher may provide a format. Add multimedia components when appropriate. Edit for grammar and mechanics. You may be asked to share your writing with the class. (W.6.2, W.6.4, W.6.5, W.6.6, W.6.7, W.6.8, RI.6.1, SL.6.5, SL.6.6, L.6.1, L.6.2, L.6.3)

  - Topics could include

    - Opinion letters to authors you have read about their books
    - Letters to editors of local newspapers, city administrators, parents, or city personnel in support of or defending local actions
    - How are personal values reflected in the friends we choose?
    - What are Fibonacci numbers or tessellations?
    - Who are the most famous women astronauts?
    - Who was the most famous mathematician?
    - Explain the class routine to a substitute

- Homework and Practice—Work with a partner to generate possible questions so that you may conduct interviews of school staff, teachers, custodians, nurse, and school board members about what they do in the school. Conduct your interviews and compile the information into an explanatory essay. You could also create a Power-

Point presentation or a video to be shared with the class. Edit your writing for grammar and mechanics. (W.6.2, W.6.4, W.6.5, W.6.6, SL.6.1, SL.6.5, SL.6.6, L.6.1, L.6.2, L.6.3)

- Interview a close family member: find out where and when they were born, where they grew up, went to school, jobs, how did he/she meet mom/dad, and favorite family story. Compile the details into a narrative. Add family photographs to power point presentations or other appropriate visuals. (W.6.3)

- Homework and Practice—Write a position paper that evaluates the author's use of narrative elements and literary devices. Cite specific examples from the text to support your opinion. (W.6.2, W.6.4, W.6.5, W.6.6, RI.6.1, RI.6.3, L.6.1, L.6.2, L.6.3, L.6.5)
- Homework and Practice—Write directions for someone else explaining how to use commas, parentheses, and dashes; vary sentence patterns; and how to use Greek or Latin affixes and roots as clues to the meaning of new words. (W.6.2, W.6.10, L.6.2a, L.6.3a, L.6.4b)
- Homework and Practice—Conduct research to answer the question: Where would I go for the ultimate vacation and what would I do there? Present your findings in a presentation for the class. Include multimedia and visual displays. Edit your presentation for grammar and mechanics. (W.6.2, W.6.4, W.6.5, W.6.6, SL.6.6, L.6.1, L.6.2, L.6.3)

  - Additional topics could include
    - The best job in the world would be _____ .
    - If I were in sixth grade during the Civil War, my life would be so different.

- Compare and Contrast—Write a bio-poem for a favorite author or person you have read about. You may need to do a little research about your author or person. Get with a partner who wrote about the same author or person of interest and compare and contrast the information in your bio-poems. Complete a Venn diagram to illustrate the similarities and differences. (W.6.3, SL.6.1)
- Cooperative Learning—Work with a partner or in a small group to write and illustrate your own fractured fairy tale. Select a fairy tale and discuss the changes that should be made. Create a T-chart to help you organize your details. On the left side list the main characters, setting, time, narrator, or speaker, point of view, the problem or conflict, one key detail, and the ending of the original story. On the right-hand side, write out the changes you are making with possible suggestions for illustrations. Include dialogue and descrip-

tive language. Edit your story for grammar and mechanics. Publish and record your story for classmates or to be shared with other grade levels. (W.6.3, W.6.4, W.6.5, W.6.6, W.6.10, SL.6.1, SL.6.6, L.6.1, L.6.2, L.6.3, L.6.5)

- Role-play your fractured fairy tale for classmates or other grade levels.

- Cooperative Learning—Work with a partner or in a small group to write your own circular story—stories that begin and end in the same place. Start with an event you record on a circle graphic organizer. Add three more events so that you end back at the beginning. For example, event one: go to the store to buy pizza. Event two: friends come and stay for dinner. Event three: friends are so hungry they eat all of your pizza. Event four: friends go home. You should now be back at the beginning so event five is: you go to the store to buy pizza. Include dialogue and descriptive language. Edit your story for grammar and mechanics. Publish and record your story for classmates or to be shared with other grade levels. (W.6.3, W.6.4, W.6.5, W.6.6, W.6.10, SL.6.1, SL.6.6, L.6.1, L.6.2, L.6.3, L.6.5)
- Cooperative Learning—Work with a partner or small group to write your own frame story—a story with in a story. You as the storyteller must be connected to your story, and the connection will be revealed at the end of the story you tell. For example, pretend you are a camp counselor and you tell a story to your campers about a mysterious event that happened to a young child in that summer camp many years ago, something that resulted in a jagged scar on the forehead. At the end of the story the counselor tells, the counselor pushes back her hair from around her face and everyone realizes the mysterious event happened to you (the counselor)! Include dialogue and descriptive language. Edit your story for grammar and mechanics. Publish your story and share it with classmates. (W.6.3, W.6.4, W.6.5, W.6.6, SL.6.6, L.6.1, L.6.2, L.6.3, L.6.5)
- Nonlinguistic Representations—Role-play a day in the life of a favorite character. Create a content web or outline or other appropriate organizer to organize your thoughts and list any supportive materials you will need. Practice your presentation before you present it to the class. (W.6.3, SL.6.1, SL.6.6)

    - Role-play what happened to your character after the story was over.
    - Role-play an event that happened to someone else.
    - Prepare a skit to entitled "A Day in the Life of ____" and present it to the class.
    - Write a song, rap, or poem.

- Questions—Ask questions to spark interest in narrative writing. You might post several questions on chart paper and post around the classroom. Students read and respond to the questions as they walk the room. Students can use the information on the charts in their writing. (W.6.3)
  - What if you could run the school for the day?
  - What if you won the lottery?
  - What if you your pets could talk?
  - What if you were the principal/teacher for the day?
  - What if you could travel to anywhere in the world?
  - What if you could be the president?
- Homework and Practice—Write an autobiography. To begin, take notes on a content web, outline, or other graphic organizer, about special events you want to include in your autobiography. To enhance your writing, create a table of contents and add other features such as fact boxes, charts, maps, or diagrams. Add headings and subheadings where appropriate. Your teacher may have a specific format for you to follow. Revise and edit your writing for grammar and mechanics. (W.6.3, W.6.4, W.6.5, W.6.6, L.6.1, L.6.2, L.6.3)
  - Create a life graph timeline for your autobiography.
- Homework and Practice—Write an acrostic poem to develop a real or imagined experience or event. (W.6.3)
  - Try the acrostic poem creator: http://www.netrover.com/~kingskid/poetry/acrostictrace.html
- Homework and Practice—Select a character or real person you have read about. Write the name of the character or person down the side of a page. Write a poem, either free verse or rhyming, about the character or person. The first word of each line begins with the letter at the beginning of the line. The poem can be done as a class exercise, with students taking turns adding a line one at a time, or it can be written in small groups or by individuals. Poems can be shared in the class. (W.6.3, SL.6.1, SL.6.6)
  - If all students write about the same character or person, poems could be compared and contrasted in class discussions.
  - Write a poem about a person who has been important in your life.
- Homework and Practice—As poems are written about various topics throughout the year, make copies of them and create a class

anthology of poetry. Illustrations may also be added to poems. (W.6.3, W.6.4, W.6.6)
- Homework and Practice—As you read, create and complete a table to identify historical fiction events. Your table should include titles, main characters, setting, two to three main events and state whether the story is told in first or third person. When your table has several entries, look at the titles and decide which you liked best and in what person the stories were told. Which stories helped you make the connection to the real event and helped you better comprehend what happened and why. Write a position paper to explain your choice. (W.6.3, W.6.4, W.6.5, W.6.6, L.6.1, L.6.2, L.6.3)
- Homework and Practice—Write a short story about one event in your life. Include setting, plot, dialogue, characters, details, and a happy ending. Use concrete details and descriptive language; use first or third person. Add appropriate visuals. Edit your story for grammar and mechanics. You may be asked to share your story with the class. Publish your story in a class story book. (W.6.3, W.6.4, W.6.5, W.6.6, W.6.8, SL.6.1, SL.6.5, SL.6.6, L.6.1, L.6.2, L.6.3, L.6.5)
  - Record your story with appropriate sound effects and share it with other students or grade levels.
  - Life is full of surprises. Identify and describe a time you were surprised.
- Homework and Practice—Write your own mystery. Create a main character. Choose and describe an interesting setting; create a mysterious event or puzzle to be solved. What events will happen to your character as he tries to solve the mystery? What will your cliffhanger be? How will your character solve the puzzle? Brainstorm ideas with a partner and jot ideas on a content web to help you organize your thoughts. Add visuals to your writing. Edit your mystery for grammar and mechanics and be prepared to share your mystery with the class. Publish your mystery. (W.6.3, W.6.4, W.6.5, W.6.6, W.6.8, SL.6.1, SL.6.5, SL.6.6, L.6.1, L.6.2, L.6.3, L.6.5)
  - Role-play your mystery with classmates adding multimedia components and visuals where appropriate.
- Homework and Practice—Pretend you are a fifth grade student posing as a sixth grade student. Write a story entitled, "My Secret Life as a Sixth Grade Student." Write a story that depicts life in middle school as a sixth grader to dispel any rumors to fifth graders. Add visuals to your writing. Edit your story for grammar and mechanics and be prepared to share your story with a class of fifth grade students. Publish your story in a class anthology. (W.6.3,

W.6.4, W.6.5, W.6.6, W.6.8, SL.6.1, SL.6.5, SL.6.6, L.6.1, L.6.2, L.6.3, L.6.5)

- Homework and Practice—Write a prequel to your favorite story. What elements of the story and characters would you need to include? What new characters would you create? Remember your prequel must end where your favorite story begins. Edit your story for grammar and mechanics. (W.6.3, W.6.4, W.6.5, W.6.6, L.6.1, L.6.2, L.6.3)
- Homework and Practice—Think about a minor character from a story, play, drama, or poem. Write the "rest of the story" for that minor character. What happened to him or her? You need to create a setting and a problem that the major character couldn't solve in the original story. Does this change the way she was seen originally? What elements of the story need to stay the same? What needs to be changed? How old is the character now? Your story should end with "and now you know the rest of the story." Write, edit, and publish your story to share with classmates or other students. (W.6.3, W.6.4, W.6.5, W.6.6, W.6.10, SL.6.6, L.6.1, L.6.2, L.6.3, L.6.5)

  - Record or role-play your story.

- Homework and Practice—Write magazine or feature articles for a class publication. Conduct research on topics of interest. Conduct interviews of experts to add interest to your articles. Edit your writing for grammar and mechanics. Your teacher may have a specific format for you to use. (W.6.3, W.6.4, W.6.5, W.6.7, W.6.10, L.6.1, L.6.2, L.6.3)
- Homework and Practice—Write a memoir poem. Create a timeline to identify several small events or many details about one major event. Use the timeline to help you organize your thoughts. Your poem may or may not rhyme. The first line should establish the theme of your poem. The next line should be the first important event or the first detail about a single event. The rest of the poem should be sequential. Edit for grammar and mechanics. (W.6.3, W.6.4, W.6.5, L.6.1, L.6.2, L.3)
- Homework and Practice—Rewrite your favorite fairy tale as a news story. Create a headline and byline. Begin with a dateline stating the location of a story, followed by a lead paragraph that tells who, what, where, when and why information. Include two more paragraphs to give further details. Edit your story for grammar and mechanics. Publish your story with at least one photograph with a caption. The photograph should have a credit line beside the photo so you know who took the photograph. (W.6.3, W.6.4, W.6.5, W.6.6, L.6.1, L.6.2, L.6.3)
- Compare and Contrast—Authors write to inform, entertain, persuade, reflect, instruct, retell or plan. Create a content web to illus-

trate the differences between the various purposes. Create a sample of each type of writing and add it to your web. (W.6.4)
- Compare and Contrast—Choose a narrative and an informational piece of writing and create a content web or other appropriate organizer to compare and contrast the two pieces with regard to development, organization and style, purpose and audiences. Discuss your results in small group or class discussions. (W.6.4, SL.6.1)
- Compare and Contrast—Create a content web to illustrate the differences in various genres. With a partner, discuss the content web to determine why authors write in specific genres. Consider the following genres for your web: autobiographies, biographies, drama, fables, fairy tales, fantasy, general nonfiction, humor, poetry, historical fiction, horror, mystery, realistic fiction, and science fiction. (W.6.4)
- Summarize—In a journal format, write summaries to describe the various formats used by authors. (W.6.4)
- Take Notes—As you read various genres, take notes about the style, organization, and purposes for writing found in each genre. (W.6.4)
- Homework and Practice—The author's point of view, belief, or stance is clearly stated in the sentence [quote the sentence]. Support or refute the author's point of view, belief, stance in an argument. Your teacher will provide a format for your writing. Edit your writing for grammar and mechanics. You may be asked to present your argument to the class. (W.6.4, W.6.1, W.6.5, W.6.6, W.6.7, SL.6.1, L.6.1, L.6.2, L.6.3)
- Homework and Practice—Write an argument to criticize a resource you used and give three suggestions to improve it. Edit your writing for grammar and mechanics. Present your argument to the class. (W.6.4, W.6.1, W.6.5, W.6.6, SL.6.1, SL.6.6, L.6.1, L.6.2, L.6.3)
- Compare and Contrast—Compare and contrast a first draft to your final draft. Explain to a partner how and why you planned, revised, edited, and rewrote the first draft to strengthen your writing. (W.6.5)
- Compare and Contrast—Conduct research into various ways to approach a topic that have been used by others. Create a web or other appropriate organizer to illustrate the various approaches. Cite each approach with title and page numbers or use a format provided by your teacher. (W.6.5, RL.6.1, RI.6.1)
- Take Notes—Take notes as you talk with peers and teachers about expanding ideas to improve your writing. (W.6.5)
- Take Notes—To improve your writing, make and note observations about things around you—the settings, people, places, events—for use in possible current or future stories or topics. (W.6.5)

Strategies and Activities for Writing 71

- Take Notes—Do research and take notes of how others have approached similar topics. (W.6.5)
- Take Notes—Create a class chart to display editing and proofreading checklist for all to use when working in small groups or as a class. The chart will also remind you of what you need to check when editing and revising your work. (W.6.5)
- Questions—Ask questions of peers and teachers when planning, revising, editing, rewriting, or trying new approaches. (W.6.5)
- Homework and Practice—Rewrite text into a different genre. You could change a memoir into a poem; a biography into a narrative story; a mystery into fantasy. Edit your writing for grammar and mechanics. Share an excerpt from both with the class to show your changes. (W.6.5, W.6.6, SL.6.1, SL.6.6, L.6.1, L.6.2, L.6.3)
    - Compare and Contrast—create a table or T-chart to show what you kept the same and what you changed.
- Take Notes—Use class or individual spreadsheets, charts or other print or digital sources to take notes. (W.6.6)
- Cooperative Learning—Interact and collaborate with others while using technology to communicate, produce, and publish. (W.6.6)
    - Write and respond to emails as allowed in your district.
    - Use online learning programs as allowed in your district.
- Homework and Practice—practice your keyboarding skills at home and at school so that you can type a minimum of three pages in a single sitting. (W.6.6)
    - Use keyboarding skills to draft, revise, edit, and publish your work.
- Homework and Practice—Use a variety of technological tools in writing. (W.6.6)
    - Use computers and scanners to create and edit documents and to add photos or images.
    - Use digital dictionaries, a thesaurus, and spell-check when writing and editing.
- Questions—When conducting research, ask a variety of relevant questions. See the stem statements in Appendix C. (W.6.7)
    - Use interviews, books, articles, photos, illustrations, and the Internet to locate and verify answers to questions.
    - Use multiple online sites and resources for your research.
- Homework and Practice—Use concise writing and several resources when responding to a prompt, refocusing the inquiry when needed. (W.6.7)

- Compare and Contrast—Compare and contrast information in print and digital resources on the same topic using a T-Chart, Venn diagram, or other appropriate organizer. Compare and contrast two or three print resources, two or three digital resources, and/or a print and a digital resource. Is the information the same? What information is different? Can you determine why the information would be different? Does one resource seem to be more credible than the other? Share your diagram with a partner or small group. (W.6.8, SL.6.1)
- Summarizing—Summarize texts from print and digital sources including only appropriate and important details. (W.6.8)
- Take Notes—Quote or paraphrase the data and conclusions of others while avoiding plagiarism; create a bibliography of references according to the format provided by your teacher. (W.6.8)
    - Remember to cite and credit downloaded materials from interactive media.
    - Note sources of information to be used in bibliography.
- Take Notes—Assess the credibility of each source. Take note of the author's qualifications and credentials. Has the author been peer reviewed? Are there clues to the author's bias? Is the information current and comparable to other sources? Does the author include a bibliography and citations? Are there mechanical errors? If using a website, is it a commercial, educational, governmental, or nonprofit site? (W.6.8)
- Cooperative Learning—When considering several resources on the same topic for a group project, divide up the resources among the group. Skim the information and taking turns, paraphrase the data and any conclusions for the group. Decide which resources you want to use based on the paraphrases. Cite your evidence for future use in your group project. (W.6.8)
- Make Predictions—Make predictions using evidence from literary or informational texts and personal knowledge when writing. (W.6.9)
- Compare and Contrast—Select two to three literary pieces that contain examples of symbolism, humor, irony, or suspense. Create a two- or three-circle Venn diagram to compare and contrast how one of the elements is used in two or three different selections. Write an essay to explain your findings. Cite textual evidence to support your analysis. Edit your writing for grammar and mechanics. (W.6.9, W.6.2, L.6.1, L.6.2, L.6.3)
- Homework and Practice—Write an essay to describe the way authors use symbolism, humor, irony or suspense, drawing evidence from literary texts to support your analysis. Edit your writing for grammar and mechanics. (W.6.9, RL.6.1, L.6.1, L.6.2, L.6.3)

Strategies and Activities for Writing

- Homework and Practice—Conduct a survey of your classmates to determine their points of view on a particular topic of interest to you. Create a poster or chart to illustrate the points of view, including yours, and any supportive evidence for each. Post the poster or chart on the wall and discuss the points and analyze the evidence in small or large group discussion. (W.6.9, SL.6.1, SL.6.6)
- Homework and Practice—Write for extended time frames, a range of tasks and purposes, and various audiences. Conduct research when necessary. Edit your writing and be prepared to present your writing to the class. (W.6.10, SL.6.1, SL.6.6, L.6.1, L.6.2, L.6.3)
    - Write a variety of short stories including myths, legends, fables, fairytales, realistic or historical fiction, or fantasy.
    - Write a biography about a relative or friend.
    - Write feature articles for a class magazine. Your teacher may provide specific topics related to your school.
    - Write various types of poetry and compile into an individual anthology. Write poems to include cinquains, circle poems, concrete poems, free verse, haiku, and limericks.

SEVEN

Grade 6 Strategies and Activities for Speaking and Listening

Choose literary or informational text from Grades 6–8 text exemplars selections or other appropriate grade level selections. Grades 6–8 text exemplars are noted with an (EX).

- Compare and Contrast—In group or class discussions, create content webs to illustrate the various perspectives of the group. Then compare and contrast the different perspectives in discussions and the graphic organizer helps each to build on the thoughts and views of the others. (SL.6.1)
- Take Notes—Use sticky notes or tags to mark texts and find information in class or group discussions. Refer to the notes or tags on the topic, text, or issue to probe and reflect on ideas under discussion. (SL.6.1)
- Take Notes—Use the two-column note format to indicate specific text citations in class notes. Put notes on the right half and citations on the left. (SL.6.1)
- Take Notes—Take notes in a format comfortable for you as you listen in group or class discussions. Formulate questions before and during presentations looking for answers in texts during discussions. (SL.6.1)
- Take Notes—Create a journal to write reflections on a daily basis on key ideas and perspectives. (SL.6.1)
- Cooperative Learning—Practice ways to "get the floor" in group or class discussions. Follow rules for collegial discussions and set goals and deadlines, defining individual roles as needed. Your teacher may have specific roles and guidelines for you to follow. (SL.6.1)

- You can use talking stones or chips—students begin discussion with three to four stones or chips and gives up one each time they add to the discussion. When stones or chips are gone, they must wait until all others have contributed. If you want to limit discussion, give one stone or chip to each student. You can also use a timekeeper to limit the length of contributions to discussions so you have time for all to contribute.
- You can also toss the ball—one student speaks. If others want to contribute, the first student tosses the ball to another student. This continues until all who want to contribute have the opportunity to do so.
- You can use playing cards to "stack the deck." Students are given a card and contribute according to their card. Begin with aces and proceed down through the deck ending with deuces.

- Use the Kagan Cooperative Learning strategy of Paraphrase Passport[1] to review key ideas and multiple perspectives. Students should get into groups of four. The first student makes comments or observations about a topic (such as why they would or would not visit the country presented) while the others listen. The next student must paraphrase what the first student said before adding his or her own comments or observations. The process continues around the group until all have paraphrased and contributed. (SL.6.1)
  - Paraphrase Passport can also be used to review key ideas expressed and demonstrate understanding of multiple perspectives in small group discussions.
  - Allow students to suggest ways to "get the floor" such as by raising hands, talk in a circle sequentially, or birthdates.
  - Allow all to contribute before changing the subject.
- Questions—Use and respond to stem questions from appendix C with elaboration and detail by making comments that contribute to the topic, text or issue under discussion. (SL.6.1)
- Homework and Practice—Read "Eleven" by Sandra Cisneros. Bring an artifact to class that is representative of something from your childhood when you were eleven—and ten, and nine, and eight, and so on. Talk about the artifact in group or class discussion, describing the role of the artifact and its importance to you growing up. (SL.6.1, SL.6.6)
- Homework and Practice—When presenting verbal arguments, use vocabulary appropriate to the argument and support the argument with relevant evidence. (SL.6.1)

- Take Notes—Note specific information gained from illustrations or graphics. Cite the page number of the illustration or graphic for easy retrieval in group or class discussion. (SL.6.2, RL.6.1, RI.6.1)
- Cooperative Learning—In small groups, take notes and discuss how the Internet, video games, media games, radio, and television entertain students today. Share the information from your group with the class as you compare and contrast ideas and thoughts in large group discussion. (SL.6.2, SL.6.1)
- Cooperative Learning—Participate in a class debate to argue the statement: Today's media has a positive (or negative) affect on middle school students. Your teacher will provide a specific format for you to follow. (SL.6.2, SL.6.1, SL.6.6)
- Cooperative Learning—Create a table with two columns labeled "Visual" and "Verbal." Label your rows "Poem," "Print," and "Audio." Read silently the poem "The Midnight Ride of Paul Revere" by Henry Wadsworth Longfellow. (You could use any other appropriate text as well.) Note on your table what you "see" or "hear" as you read silently. Then look at several images either in print or digital format of paintings or prints that depict the midnight ride. Note what you "see" and "hear" from the prints or paintings. Finally, listen to audio recordings of the poem and again note what you "see" and "hear." Discuss in small or large groups how the visuals and audio recordings help you to see and hear what happened and help you to understand the events. (SL.6.2, SL.6.1)
- Questions—Describe how important it is to have information presented in numerous ways (e.g., visually, quantitatively, orally). How well would you comprehend information if it was only presented in one way? (SL 6.2)
- Questions—What is the relationship between text and nontext? How would your learning be affected if you only had text or non-text materials? Share your thoughts with a partner or the class. (SL.6.2, SL.6.1)
- Homework and Practice—Use a SQRRR frame. Survey the chapter headings, section titles and headings, subheadings, illustrations, captions, and graphics. Reword the titles and headings into questions and predict what you will read about. Be prepared to share how the illustrations, captions, and graphics contribute to the topic, text or issue at hand. (SL.6.2, SL.6.1)
- Compare and Contrast—Create large two-circle Venn diagrams on chart paper or digitally. When listening to arguments on the same topic, document similar claims and reasons supported by evidence through class discussion. For example, assume you have a topic of school uniforms. One circle of the Venn represents those "For Uniforms" and the other circle represents those "Against Uniforms."

After the first two arguments are presented, fill in the Venn noting different reasons in the outer circles and same reasons (either for or against) in the inner section. Where do you think you will have the most information? Discuss the variety of reasons for or against the topic. Is there anything special about the center section with regard to the responses? (SL.6.3, SL.6.1)

- Summarize—Give oral summaries in small groups of arguments and specific claims, identifying the claims that are supported by reasons and evidence. (SL.6.3)
- Take Notes—After listening to presentations, look for information to speak to the credibility of the author to help determine the validity of the speaker's claims. (SL.6.3)
- Homework and Practice—In group or class discussion, delineate a speaker's argument and specific claims, distinguishing claims supported by reasons and evidence from those that are not. Create a class table or T-chart to help guide discussion. (SL.6.3)
- Homework and Practice—As you listen to presentations or media messages, identify and discuss instances of bias in the presentations or media messages. Try to determine the author's purpose in the bias. Discuss how the messages or presentations affect you as a middle school student. Teachers, there are several sites you can choose. Please check the site prior to use in the classroom as sites do change. (SL.6.3)
    - http://www.educationworld.com/a_lesson/lesson/lesson158.shtml. You can find several ideas here about lessons for on-line advertising that targets kids.
    - http://www.ehow.com/info_12102253_advertising-activities-middle-school.html
    - http://www.webenglishteacher.com/media-ads.html. This is a great list to help you find media and advertising resources.
- Homework and Practice—Prepare and present arguments to the class. Practice deductive reasoning by using a variety of mysteries for kids based on the claims and evidence in the books. Your teacher may provide a specific format for you to follow. Practice your argument in front of a mirror, friend, or family member prior to presenting in class. Use appropriate eye contact, volume, and pronunciation. (SL.6.4, SL.6.6)

    Almost Perfect Crimes: Mini-Mysteries for You to Solve by Hy Conrad (1995)

    Great Quicksolve Whodunit Puzzles: Mini-Mysteries for You to Solve by Jim Sukach (1999)

    Great Book of Whodunit Puzzles: Mini-Mysteries of You to Solve by Falcon Travis (1993)

Strategies and Activities for Speaking and Listening

CSI Expert! Forensic Science for Kids by Karen Schulz (2008)

- Homework and Practice—Prepare and present expository reports for the class that present claims and findings. (SL.6.4, SL.6.6)

  - Try topics such as

    Mysteries in History
    The Bermuda Triangle
    Orbs at the Civil War Battlefields
    The Existence of Atlantis
    Mayan Mysteries
    Who Invented the Alphabet?
    The Easter Island Statues

- Homework and Practice—Prepare and present persuasive presentations using clear and logical arguments. Your teacher will provide a format for you to follow. (SL.6.4, SL.6.6)

  - Use topics listed for writing or other appropriate topics as listed in chapter 6.

- Homework and Practice—Include multimedia components and visual displays to presentations to clarify information. (SL.6.5)

  - Search Microsoft.com for directions on how to add sound, movies, and animation to PowerPoint presentations or Word documents.

- Nonlinguistic Presentations—Role-play a scene from favorite stories or poems. (SL.6.6)

  - Memorize a specific piece of nonfiction and present a dramatic reading.

- Nonlinguistic Presentations—Record stories, poems, speeches, myths, or other appropriate readings for others to listen to. (SL.6.6)

NOTE

1. Kagan, S., & Kagan, M. (1997). *Kagan Cooperative Learning Smart Card* (pp. 2–3). San Clemente, CA: Kagan Publishing.

EIGHT

Grade 6 Strategies and Activities for Language

Choose literary or informational text from Grades 6–8 text exemplars selections or other appropriate grade-level selections. Grades 6–8 exemplars are noted with an (EX). Students work individually, as partners, small groups or as a class.

- Homework and Practice—In a journal, write sentences that include nominative, possessive, objective, and subjective pronouns. Use the sentences as examples for you to use in future writing. (L.6.1)
- Homework and Practice—Edit your writing for pronouns, punctuation and spelling. (L.6.1, L.6.2)
  - Edit writing for pronoun shifts and vague pronouns.
- Homework and Practice—Clip editorials or other examples of writing from newspapers or magazines. Edit for proper use of pronouns by circling errors. Write the sentence correctly. (L.6.1, L.6.2)
- Homework and Practice—Practice writing sentences of varying length using pronouns in the proper case. (L.6.1, L.6.2)
- Homework and Practice—Recognize variations from standard English. Read the story "The People Could Fly" by Virginia Hamilton (EX) or other stories containing dialect. Describe how dialect affects the story. A great list of possible stories can be found at http://bankstreet.edu/library/children-resources/childrens-book-lists/dialect-variation. (L.6.1e)
  - African American Stories

    The Complete Tales of Uncle Remus by Joel C. Harris (1955)

> *Bo Rabbit Smart for True: Tall Tales from the Gullah* by Priscilla Joaquith (1995)
> *Mirandy and Brother Wind* by Patricia McKissack (1988)
> *Sukey and the Mermaid* by Robert D. San Souci (1992)
> *The Cay* by Theodore Taylor (1969)

- Caribbean Stories

  > *An Island Christmas* by Lynn Joseph (1992)
  > *The Faithful Friend* by R. D. San Souci (1995)

- Spanish Stories

  > *Abuela* by Arthur Dorros (1991)
  > *Chato's Kitchen* by Gary Soto (1995)
  > *Abuelita's Heart* by Amy Cardova (1997)

- Other Regional U.S. Dialects

  > *The Jack Tales* edited by Richard Chase (1943)
  > *Across Five Aprils* by Irene Hunt (1993)
  > *Strawberry Girl* by Lois Lenski (1945)
  > *Liza Lou and the Yeller Belly Swamp* by Mercer Mayer (1976)

- Hypothesize and Test—Find various examples of sentences that use a comma, parentheses, or dash. Formulate a hypothesis based on what you observe in the sentence structure. Test your hypothesis and record and report your results. (L.6.2)
- Homework and Practice—Identify and use various forms of capitalization including headings and titles. (L.6.2)
  - Edit and correct your writing for capitalization errors.
- Homework and Practice—Create flash cards to practice spelling words. (L.6.2)
  - Edit and correct your writing for spelling errors.
- Homework and Practice—Write a variety of sentences to practice using commas and parentheses. (L.6.2)
  - Practice combining simple sentences, building on each to vary sentence length and type.
- Nonlinguistic Representations—Create a symbol or draw an image or picture to help you remember the meaning of a word. (L.6.4)
- Homework and Practice—Create a word wall for the class to use or individual card files for students to use. Write new words, noting affixes, roots, parts of speech, and the meaning as it is used in context. Note whether the word is of Greek or Latin origin. (L.6.4)

Strategies and Activities for Language 83

- Homework and Practice—Use print or digital references to determine word pronunciation, definitions, derivation, and parts of speech. (L.6.4)
- Homework and Practice—Create a chart on the wall to identify words of Greek and Latin affixes and roots. Add to the chart as you identify new words. The chart should have columns for prefixes, suffixes, roots, and root definition, origin, and examples. Add new words to the column for examples. Your teacher may provide specific affixes and roots to look for but some common ones are listed below. (L.6.4)

    Prefixes: dis, in, il, im, ir, inter, micro, non, super, trans, un
    Suffixes: age, ant, ed, ent, eous, es, ing, ious, ic, ity, ize, ous, s, ty
    Roots: aud, bene, chron, hydr, phon, port, scrib, script, spect, tele, therm, vac

- Homework and Practice—Interpret personification in context. Read a variety of text and identify what is personified and explain how it is an example of personification. (L.6.5)

    Pinocchio (Puffin Classics) by Carlo Collodi (1996)
    Charlotte's Web by E. B. White (2004)
    Miss Hickory by Carolyn Sherwin Bailey (1977)
    Lady and the Tramp by Teddy Slater (1993)
    Pout Pout Fish by Deborah Diesen (2008)
    Miraculous Journey of Edward Tulane by Kate DiCamillo (2009)
    Hitty, Her First Hundred Years by Rachel Field (1998)

- Homework and Practice—Use similes and metaphors in sentences to make comparisons. Write a sentence with a simile. Change the simile into a metaphor. Explain how the meaning changes in the two sentences. Share with a partner. (L.6.5)
- Homework and Practice—Choose a dialectical word from one story and try to locate similar words in other dialects. You may want to use words that have the same meaning or connotation. Use online dictionaries or a thesaurus to help you. Share your words with the class. (L.6.5c)
- Homework and Practice—Create lists of analogies to understand the relationship between words. As you read, identify examples of word relationships. You can create a chart or other graphic organizer to illustrate the relationships of cause/effect, part to whole, and item to category. Discuss the relationships and how the analogy explains the relationship. (L.6.5)
    - Cause/Effect—
        - Tornado is to destruction as drought is to famine.
        - Earthquake is to tsunami as heavy rain is to flood.

- Part to Whole—
    - Petal is to flower as pages are to a book.
    - Leaves are to trees as bricks are to a house.
- Item to Category—
    - Oaks are to trees as rings are to jewelry.
    - Apples are to fruits as Monopoly is to games.
- Take Notes—As you read in all subject areas, note new terms associated with that particular subject area. Create a class chart for new terms and definitions. Use the words or phrases appropriately. (L.6.6)
    - You could also create vocabulary notebooks that also contain a picture that describes the term and definition so it will be easier for you to remember both.

NINE
Grade 6 Strategies and Activities for Reading Literacy in History and Social Studies

Choose literary or informational text from Grades 6–8 text exemplars selections or other appropriate grade level selections. Grade 6–8 exemplars are noted with an (EX). You may also select primary sources from the sites listed here. The standards are grade-span in nature, but the text suggestions and activities are on a Grade 6 level.

PRIMARY SOURCES WEBSITES

(http://www.lib.berkeley.edu/instruct/guides/primarysourcesontheweb.html)

- Ad*Access, http://scriptorium.lib.duke.edu:80/adaccess/—advertisements from the United States and Canada from 1911 to 1955
- American Civil War Homepage, http://sunsite.utk.edu/civil-war—images, documents, and photographs from the Civil War
- American Memory, http://lcweb2.loc.gov/ammem/—digitized collections of documents, moving pictures and text, photographs, sound
- American Studies Web, http://www.georgetown.edu/crossroads/asw/archives.html—general American history resources
- Bancroft Library, http://bancroft.berkeley.edu/collections/—wide variety of special collections
- Documenting the American South, http://docsouth.unc.edu—Southern literature, slave narratives, first-person narratives

- Edsitement, http://edsitement.neh.gov/websites.html?all—history, language arts, and social studies sites maintained by the National Endowment for the Humanities
- Euro Docs, http://eudocs.lib.byu.edu/—historical documents from western Europe
- HarpWeek, http://app.harpweek.com/—*Harper's Weekly* from 1857 to 1865
- Historical Newspapers Online, http://historynews.chadwyck.com/—various newspaper articles from 1790 to 1980
- History Matters, http://historymatters.gmu.edu/—first-person narratives of average Americans
- Internet Library of Early Journals, http://ww.bodley.ox.ac.uk/ilej/—eighteenth- and nineteenth-century journals
- Valley of the Shadow: Living the Civil War in Pennsylvania and Virginia, http://jefferson.village.virginia.edu/vshadow/vshadow.html—lists of additional websites for studying the Civil War
- U.S. Historical Documents Online, http://w3.one.net/%7Emweiler/ushda/list.htm—historical documents from the time of Columbus through the Civil Rights Act of 1991
- World War II Resources, http://www.ibiblio.org/pha

STRATEGIES AND ACTIVITIES

- Homework and Practice—Read a variety of history and social studies texts. Cite textual evidence to support analysis of primary and secondary sources using a specific format your teacher will provide. (RLHS.6-8.1)
- Compare and Contrast—Create a list of primary and secondary sources. In class discussion, analyze how the two types of sources are the same, how they are different, the kind of information each source provides, and state the benefits of each source. (RLHS.6-8.2)
- Summarize—Read a variety of primary and secondary sources to determine the central ideas of or information in the source. Write accurate summaries of primary and secondary sources distinct from prior knowledge or opinions. (RLHS.6-8.2, WHST.6-8.10)
- Take Notes—Read through primary or secondary sources and take notes on specific details found in the documents. Include citations in your notes so you do not have to look them up again. Follow the format given to you by your teacher. Remember that primary sources include birth certificates, business receipts, court records, diaries, firsthand newspaper accounts, journals, letters, maps, photos, and transcripts of interviews or speeches. Secondary sources include biographies, book and movie reviews, encyclope-

dias, essays, news articles, public television documentaries, and social studies texts. (RLHS.6-8.2)
- Cooperative Learning—In order to break up large quantities of text to determine central ideas and information, get students into groups of four or more to do a Kagan Cooperative Learning structure called Jigsaw.[1] Divide students into groups and give each group a chunk of information. That group reads, discusses, and gets answers to questions on the information to become "experts." When each group "knows" their information, they then divide into other groups to share their portion of what each learned. (RLHS.6-8.2, SL.6.1)
    - For example, give each student a colored chip or slip of paper. Ask them to get into groups so that the group is made up of different colors with no duplicate colors. Students will then get into groups of the same color, such as all blues together, reds together, etc. You will need to decide the numbers of colors and groups prior to grouping. Hand out the chunked material to be learned. When students are ready, direct them to get back into their original group and have them share their information. You will also need to direct the order of the sharing when using colors.
    - You can also create groups using playing cards aces through ten. Hand out your chunks accordingly so that the first part goes to the aces, the second goes to the deuces, the third to the threes, and so on. This makes sharing in the group much easier.
    - Students will summarize the information to give to the original group.
- Homework and Practice—Read a variety of text to identify key steps in a text's description of how a process related to history/social studies. Create a graphic organizer such as a content web or timeline or flow chart to illustrate the steps. Have students share their processes with the class. (RLHS.6-8.3, RLHS.6-8.10, SL.6.1, SL.6.6)
    - How to become a U.S. citizen

        How to Become a US Citizen 6th Edition: A Step-By-Step Guidebook for Self Instruction by Sally Navarro (2001)

    - How to become an FBI agent

        How to Become an FBI Agent by William Thomas (2009)

    - How a bill becomes law

From Inspiration to Legislation: How an Idea Becomes a Bill by Amy Black (2006)

Easy Simulations: How a Bill Becomes a Law: A Complete Toolkit with Background Information, Primary Sources and More by Pat Luce and Holly Joyner (2008)

- How to register to vote

    http://registertovote.org

- How to open a checking account

    http://www.ehow.com/how_2814_open-bank-account.html

    Everything Kids' Money Book by Brette McWhorter Sember (2008)

- How to run for public office

    How to Become an Elected Official by Mike Bonner (2000)
    How to Run for Political Office and Win by Melanie Williamson (2011)
    Running for Public Office by Sarah De Capua (2002)

- How to be a leader in student government

    The Essential Student Government Guide by Eric Williams (2008)

- How to become an entrepreneur

    How to Run a Lemonade Stand by Russell Cope (2013)
    How to Become an Entrepreneurial Kid by Dianne Linderman (2011)

- How to build your own country

    How to Build Your Own Country by Valerie Wyatt (2009)

- Questions—So students can gain deeper understanding of words and phrases in context, create a game of "Ask Me Three." Students should define the words and phrases first. The teacher then asks three questions and the student or small groups of students respond. You might wish to let students create the questions to strengthen their ability to ask higher order questions. (RLHS.6-8.4)

    - How would you describe the relationship to/between ____ and ____?
    - How is ____ related to ____?
    - What would be a good example of ____?
    - Which clues from context helped you to understand the meaning of the word/phrase?

Strategies and Activities for Reading Literacy in History and Social Studies 89

- How would you classify ___?
- Homework and Practice—Have students create term and definition flashcards or add to their vocabulary notebooks or card files. (RLHS.6-8.4)
  - Create word search puzzles where students identify the terms based on the definition or short definitions based on the terms.
  - Create Vocabulary Bingo cards with terms in the Bingo squares. Teacher calls out a definition and students mark the square, attempting to make a "bingo." If definitions are or can be made brief, use definitions in the bingo squares and call out the terms. (http://www.ehow.com/list_6120736_middle-school-vocabulary-activities.html)
  - Create *Jeopardy!* game questions based on the terms and definitions. Use the term in the *Jeopardy!* squares and have students ask the question based on the definition.
- Homework and Practice—Create a concept web. In each circle of the web, write one vocabulary word or phrase related to your topic. Branching off from each circle will be the definition of the word or phrase and additional information to show how it is related to the topic. (RLHS.6-8.4)
- Homework and Practice—Use the following texts or other grade-appropriate texts to practice determining informational text structure. This list was compiled by Carol Simoneau. (RLHS.6-8.5)
  - Sequential—

    The Amazing Life of Benjamin Franklin by James Cross Giblin (2000)
    Ice Cream by William Jasperson (1988)
    Sugaring Time by Kathryn Lasky (1983)
    Castle by David Macaulay (1977)
    The Buck Stops Here by Alice Provensen (1990)
    My Place by Nadia Wheatley (1992)

  - Comparative—

    Merry Ever After: The Story of Two Medieval Weddings by Joe Lasker (1977)
    Outside and Inside Trees by Sandra Markle (1993)
    The Inside-Outside Book of Washington, D.C. by Roxy Munro (2001)
    The Great Fire by Jim Murphy (2010)
    People by Peter Spier (1988)

- Causal—

    Why Mosquitoes Buzz in People's Ears by Verna Aardema (1992)
    Conestoga Wagons by R Ammon (2000)
    If You Give a Mouse a Cookie by Laura Joffe Numeroff (2010)
    The Old Red Rocking Chair by Phyllis Root (1992)
    Nettie's Trip South by Ann Turner (1995)
    A New Coat for Anna by Harriet Ziefert (1988)

- Compare and Contrast—Create a three-circle Venn diagram to compare and contrast signal words that illustrate how a text presents information in nonfiction text written sequentially, comparatively, and causally. Share your diagram with a partner and compare. Locate several signal words in a text you are currently reading to determine how information is presented in it. Will you always have words to indicate sequential order? (RLHS.6-8.5)
- Compare and Contrast—Identify texts on the same topic that present information differently (sequentially, comparatively, causally). Write an essay to compare and contrast one text structure to another text structure with regard to the information presented. (RLHS.6-8.5)
- Nonlinguistic Representations—Draw pictures to represent a sequence of events, comparison or cause and effect relationship in history. (RLHS.6-8.5)
- Nonlinguistic Representations—Create comic strip frames of five to eight sections to illustrate an event in your current classroom social studies or history text. Cut the frames apart and let a partner sequence the events. Signal words may or may not be included. (RLHS.6-8.5)
- Nonlinguistic Representations—Create historical event timelines using illustrations or symbols. (RLHS.6-8.5)
- Questions—Use stem statements to help develop questions when working with information presented in texts. (RLHS.6-8.5)

    - Sequential Questions—
        - What events or steps are listed?
        - Is the order of events important?
        - Can the order be changed and not affect the event?
        - What happens if the order of events is changed?
        - What is the time span of events?
        - What is being explained by the events?
    - Comparative Questions—
        - What is being compared?
        - How are the events or people alike?

Strategies and Activities for Reading Literacy in History and Social Studies   91

- How are they different?
- Causal Questions—
  - What happened first?
  - What happened as a result?
  - Why did the event happen?
  - How did the event happen?
  - How did people react to the event or consequences of the event?
- Homework and Practice—Conduct a scavenger hunt for examples of text written in sequential, comparative or causal format. Search textbooks, newspapers, magazines, journals, and other nonfiction texts in your classroom and/or library. Jot down the name and page number of the texts. Which format did you find the most examples of? Can you explain why? (RLHS.6-8.5)
- Homework and Practice—Collect several copies of the comics from the daily and weekend newspapers. Cut the comics into separate frames, putting each comic into an envelope. Direct students to look at the frames and put into sequential order. Without words, how do you know you have the correct order? Work individually or with a partner. (RLHS.6-8.5, SL.6.6)
- Homework and Practice—As a daily or weekly activity, write one part of a cause/effect sentence on the board. Write the cause and let students suggest reasonable effects, or write the effect and ask for reasonable causes. (RLHS.6-8.5)
- Homework and Practice—Look outside the classroom for cause and effect relationships. As you see them, jot them down and share with a partner or the class. Be able to state the cause and the effect. (RLHS.6-8.5)
  - A woman donated Civil War photos to the museum to complete their collection.
  - The candidate received 55 percent of the vote so he won the election.
- Questions—To help determine an author's purpose or point of view of a primary source, consider a variety of questions. Look at a primary source with a partner and try to answer the questions to help you determine purpose or point of view. (RLHS.6-8.6, SL.6.1)
  - Was the text handwritten, published, or printed?
  - What type and quality of paper was used? You may have to do some additional research to determine this.
  - What type of font was used if it was published?
  - Are there special images, pictures or borders on the document?

- How is the information arranged?
- Does the text appear to be a personal letter or a document that was meant to persuade?
- For whom was the document created?

- Homework and Practice—Look at a variety of advertisements throughout history to help determine author's purpose and point of view. Advertisements are good resources to use to look for loaded language as well as inclusion or avoidance of particular facts. Use the website for Ad*Access, http://scriptorium.lib.duke.edu:80/adaccess. Create a class chart to help you determine purpose and point of view. The chart should have columns for the name of the ad, loaded words, inclusion of facts, and avoidance of facts. Each student should analyze an ad, complete the chart based on information from the ad, create a statement of author's purpose and/or point of view and then share the chart and statement with a partner or the class. (RLHS.6-8.6, SL.6.1)
- Nonlinguistic Representations—Individually or in small groups, students create tables, charts, graphs, models, or diagrams to represent quantitative or technical information presented in words found in science or technical subjects text. Students share representations with the class. (RLHS.6-8.7, SL.6.1)
  - Add tables, charts, graphs, models or diagrams to individual or group presentations.
- Take Notes—Create a class table or chart with four columns—one each for the name of the source (newspaper, magazine, editorial, letter to the editor, journal article, or textbook selection), facts, opinions, and reasoned judgments. As a class, look at various sources to determine the facts, opinions, and reasoned judgments. Be able to justify how you classified the statement. Make selections from those listed or other grade-appropriate text. Please check sources for appropriateness prior to classroom use. (RLHS.6-8.8, SL.6.1)

  American Girl
  Discovery Girls
  Girl's Life
  Junior Scholastic Grades 6–8 for social studies and current events
  National Geographic for Kids
  Sports Illustrated for Kids
  http://www.dogonews.com
  http://www.gogonews.com
  http://www.headlinespot.com/for/kids
  http://www.newspaperforkids.com
  http://www.teachingkidsnews.com
  http://www.timeforkids.com

- Take Notes—Analyze the relationship between a primary and secondary source on the same topic. Choose a topic of interest. Check the web for primary sources on your topic. Identify three primary and locate actual or copies of the sources. Then identify and locate three secondary resources. Research each and take notes as to specific information found in each. Jot down a citation for the information you find to refer to later. Describe in class discussion how the primary sources are related to the secondary sources with regard to the types and reliability of information found in each. (RLHS.6-8.9, RLHS.6-8.1, SL.6.1)
- Take Notes—As a class, create a chart to list primary and secondary sources. Create a graphic organizer to help compare and contrast how the items on each list are the same, different, and what kinds of information can be found. Write a class conclusion to state the benefits of using primary and secondary sources. (RLHS.6-8.9, SL.6.1)
    - Primary sources—birth certificates, census records, court records, diaries, first hand newspaper accounts, journals, letters, photographs, receipts, transcripts of interviews or speeches, etc.
    - Secondary sources—biographies, book or movie reviews, encyclopedia entries, essays, newspaper articles, public television documentaries, social studies texts, etc.
- Hypothesize and Test—Research a historical event of interest. With a partner or in a small group, create a hypothesis based on the event and use primary and secondary sources to support or contradict your hypothesis. Cite all sources. Present your hypothesis and findings to the class. (RLHS.6-8.9, RLHS.6-8.1, SL.6.1)
- Questions—When considering primary and secondary sources on the same topic, ask to answer a variety of questions. (RLHS.6-8.9)
    - Was the author of the document present at the event? If so, how long after the event was the information recorded?
    - When was the secondary source written?
    - Do the secondary sources or other primary sources support or contradict the information?
    - Did the author of either the primary or secondary source have reasons to be honest or dishonest?
    - Who are the intended audiences of the sources?
    - What is the importance of the secondary source?
    - Is there a connection between the authors of the two sources? If so, what? If not, what is the interest of the secondary author?
    - Why was the secondary source written?

- What questions are raised after you analyze the primary and the secondary sources?

NOTE

1. Kagan, S., & Kagan, M. (1997). *Kagan Cooperative Learning Smart Card* (pp. 2–3). San Clemente, CA: Kagan Publishing.

TEN
Grade 6 Strategies and Activities for Reading Literacy in Science and Technical Subjects

Choose literary or informational text from Grades 6–8 text exemplars selections or other appropriate grade level selections. Grades 6–8 exemplars are noted with an (EX). The standards are grade-span in nature, but the text suggestions and activities are on a Grade 6 level.

- Compare and Contrast—Compare and contrast conclusions in texts on the same topic. Create a Venn diagram or other appropriate graphic organizer to illustrate same and different conclusions. Share the organizer with a partner and discuss why the conclusions may or may not differ. (RLST.6-8.2, SL.6.6)
- Summarize—Write accurate summaries of text distinct from prior knowledge or opinions. Summaries may be shared with the class. (RLST.6-8.2, WHST.6-8.2, SL.6.1)
- Nonlinguistic Representations—Create drawings on posters to illustrate central ideas of a text. (RLST.6-8.2)
    - Create a model to show a key concept.
    - Design a series of drawings or diagrams to illustrate the central ideas.
- Homework and Practice—Read a variety of texts based on science and technical topics. Determine the central ideas or conclusions of a text. Jot down the title and author of the text and state the ideas and conclusions in a reading journal. Cite evidence to support your analysis. (RLST.6-8.2, RLST.6-8.1)
- Compare and Contrast—Compare and contrast multistep procedures when carrying out experiments. Choose a topic such as how

to bake bread from scratch. Locate a recipe (the procedures) for baking bread. Write the steps out on a T-chart. Find another recipe similar to the first one and write those steps out on the other side of the T-chart. Consider the directions, temperatures, measurements, etc. Write an essay that details the similarities and differences. Consider why there are differences in the recipes with regard to procedures and measurements and state your conclusion in your essay. (RLST.6-8.3, WHST.6-8.2)

- Other topics include making pudding (instant and cooked), rock candy, soap bubble shapes, volcanoes; poke a stick or needle through a balloon. Check science experiment resources for other topics.

- Homework and Practice—Read a variety of science and technical subject texts. Choose and follow a multistep procedure to carry out experiments, take measurements, or perform technical tasks. Choose procedures from the texts listed or other grade-appropriate texts. (RLST.6-8.3, RLST.6-8.10)

    Hands-On Science Mysteries for Grades 3–6: Standards-Based Inquiry Investigations by James Robert Taris (2006)
    Help! I'm Teaching Middle School Science by C. Jill Swango and Sally Bowles Steward (2002)
    Information Literacy and Technology Research Projects: Grades 6–9 by Norma Heller (2001)
    PowerPoint for Teachers: Dynamic Presentations and Interactive Classroom Projects (K–12) by Ellen Finkelstein and Pavel Samsonov (2007)
    Science Experiments You Can Eat (Revised Edition) by Vicki Cobb (1984)
    Science Methods Investigation: A Step-by-Step Guide for School Students by Schyrlet Cameron, Carolyn Craig, and Sherryl Soutec (2010)
    Sewing School: 21 Sewing Projects Kids Will Love to Make by Andria Lisle and Amie Plumley (2010)
    Summer Bridge Activities, Grades 6–7 by Frankie Long, Leland Graham, and Katie Fields (1998)
    32 Quick and Fun Content Area Comprehension Activities for Middle School by Lynn Van Gorp (2006)

- Homework and Practice—Conduct research on how-to topics of interest. Follow multistep procedures to create or develop your topic. Work in small groups to complete your task and present your how-to project to the class. (RLST.6-8.3, SL.6.1)

    - Design a class webpage with text images and hyperlinks.

- Create a webpage for a significant person from social studies, science, or a technology inventor.
- Produce a commercial using Movie Maker.
- Create a travel documentary using PowerPoint.
- Plan and produce a podcast.

- Homework and Practice—Add new words and phrases to a vocabulary journal or card file. Check words for affixes and roots and determine whether the word is Greek or Latin in origin. Discuss with a partner what you think the word means; then use print or digital resources to define the word. Is there a synonym or antonym? Use a thesaurus to check for both. Write a sentence using the new word in your journal or card file. Add an illustration or diagram to help remember the word. (RLST.6-8.4)
- Homework and Practice—Create flashcards with terms on one side and definitions as the word is used in context to the other. (RLST.6-8.4)
- Homework and Practice—Create crossword puzzles with terms and definitions. Share the puzzles with a partner or as a class activity. (RLST.6-8.4)
- Homework and Practice—Create a question of the day related to symbols, terms, and domain-specific words and phrases. Post questions on the board adding new questions each day. For example: What is the definition of ____? Does the word remind you of another term? How is it related to ____? What would be the opposite of ____? Where would you find an example of ____? (RLST.6-8.4)
- Homework and Practice—Create a class classification chart and add words and phrases as they are learned so students begin to have a better understanding of the different sciences. Create columns for Life Science, Physical Science, Earth Science, Scientific Inquiry, and Technology. If the word or phrase fits in more than one column, add it and discuss why it would be acceptable to list in all that apply. (RLST.6-8.4, SL.6.1)
- Compare and Contrast—Authors of science and technical subject textbooks generally organize texts in a specific manor appropriate to the content. Authors will structure texts in formats of compare and contrast, cause and effect, sequence, problem and solutions and description. Many times authors will use multiple structures. Compare and contrast a narrative text to a science or technical subject text in an essay. Create a Venn diagram first to determine how the texts are similar and different. Use the organizer to write your essay. Edit your writing for grammar and mechanics. (RLST.6-8.5, WHST.6-8.2, L.6.1, L.6.2, L.6.3)
- Summaries—Write summaries of texts for each type of structure. (RLST.6-8.5, WHST.6-8.2)

- Nonlinguistic Representations—Read a science or technical subject text. Create an illustrated diagram, concept web, or other graphic organizer to show how the major sections of the text contribute to the whole and the understanding of the topic. Share and discuss the organizers with the class. (RLST.6-8.5, SL.6.1)
    - Draw a series of pictures or create a timeline with pictures to illustrate sequence.
- Cooperative Learning—Consider texts where authors use multiple structures. In groups of four, read a selection or text, noting structure signal words. Create a group table with headings that include title of the text, compare/contrast, cause/effect, sequence, problem/solution, and description. As you read, write down the signal words in the appropriate columns and the page numbers where the words were found for quick reference. Discuss in your group which structure was used most and why the author chose to use more than one structure? Does it help or hurt your comprehension? The group should formulate an answer, write it down and be prepared to share it with the class. (RLST.6-8.5, SL.6.1, SL.6.6)
    - Checkout the list of texts at emilykissner.blogspot.com that details texts and specific text structures. Multiple structure texts include

        Face to Face with Dolphins by Flip Nicklin (2007)
        Frogs: Strange and Wonderful by Laurence Pringle (2012)
        Leo the Snow Leopard by Craig Hatkoff (2010)
        Saving the Ghost of the Mountain by Sy Montgomery (2009)
        The Secret Life of a Snowflake by Kenneth Libbrecht (2010)
- Cooperative Learning—Divide the class into teams and scavenger hunt for specific examples of text structure. Students should look through magazines, newspapers, textbooks and nonfiction books. There needs to be enough resources for students to locate at least one example of each text structure. (RLST.6-8.5, SL.6.1)
- Questions—When analyzing the structure used by an author, there are many questions you can ask to help deepen the meaning of the text. (RLST.6-8.5)
    - Comparison and Contrast—
        - What did the author use in the comparison?
        - Were analogies used and how?
        - What are the similarities and differences?
        - Why did the author compare ____ to ____?
        - What signal words designate the organization as comparison and contrast?

- What are the major sections of the text?
- How do the sections contribute to the whole of the text or selection?
- How do they help you understand the topic?
- What questions do you still have?
- Why do you think the author chose this organizational format?

- Cause and Effect—
  - What event is described?
  - What are the causes discussed?
  - What are the effects discussed?
  - How did you make the distinction between the cause(s) and the effect(s)?
  - What are the major sections of the text?
  - How do the sections contribute to the whole of the text or selection?
  - How do they help you understand the topic?
  - What questions do you still have?
  - Why do you think the author chose this organizational format?

- Sequence—
  - What event is sequenced?
  - What are three to five events the author shared?
  - What is the main event in the sequence? How do you know?
  - What words or phrases were used to show sequence?
  - What are the major sections of the text?
  - How do the sections contribute to the whole of the text or selection?
  - How do they help you understand the topic?
  - What questions do you still have?
  - Why do you think the author chose this organizational format?

- Problem/Solution—
  - What is the problem?
  - What statement(s) from the selection explain(s) the problem?
  - What is the solution presented by the author?
  - What other solutions might the author have presented?
  - What are the major sections of the text?
  - How do the sections contribute to the whole of the text or selection?

- How do they help you understand the topic?
- What questions do you still have?
- Why do you think the author chose this organizational format?

• Description—

- What does the author describe? What images do you "see" in your mind's eye?
- What are the characteristics of the ____ that the author shared?
- What other characteristics would you share about the ____?
- Which signal words helped you to identify the selection as description?
- What are the major sections of the text?
- How do the sections contribute to the whole of the text or selection?
- How do they help you understand the topic?
- What questions do you still have?
- Why do you think the author chose this organizational format?

• Homework and Practice—Checkout the list of texts at emilykissner.blogspot.com that details texts and specific text structures. Some of these texts may be at younger levels but are still useful to teach the structures. (RLST.6-8.5)

- Compare and Contrast—

    Are You a Snail? by Judy Allen (2003)
    Butterfly or Moth? How Do You Know? by Melissa Stewart (2011)
    Frog or Toad? How Do You Know? by Melissa Stewart (2011)
    Nathan of Yesteryear and Michael of Today by Brian Heinz (2006)
    Shark or Dolphin? How Do You Know? by Melissa Stewart (2011)
    What's the Difference between an Alligator and a Crocodile by Lisa Bullard (2010)
    What's the Difference between a Leopard and a Cheetah? by Lisa Bullard (2009)

- Cause and Effect—

    Energy Makes Things Happen by Kimberly Bradley (2002)
    Extreme Animals by Nicola Davies (2006)

Just the Right Size: Why Big Animals Are Big . . . by Nicola Davies (2009)
Living Sunlight: How Plants Bring the Earth Life by Molly Bang (2009)
Mysterious Messages by Gary Blackwood (2009)
Unsolved History: Enigmatic Events by Gary Blackwood (2005)

- Sequence—

  A House Spider's Life by John Himmelman (2000)
  A Puffin's Year by Katherine Zecca (2007)
  The Amazing Impossible Erie Canal by Cheryl Harness (1999)
  Flute's Journey by Lynne Cherry (1997)
  Looking at Glass through the Ages by Bruce Koscielniak (2006)
  Owen and Mzee: The Language of Friendship by Isabella Hatkoff (2007)
  Trapped by the Ice: Shakelton's Amazing Antarctic Adventure by Michael McCurdy (2002)

- Problem and Solution—

  A Place for Birds by Melissa Stewart (2009)
  A Place for Butterflies by Melissa Stewart (2006)
  Falcons Nest on Skyscrapers by Priscilla Jenkins
  The Secret of the Yellow Death by Suzanne Jurmain (2009)
  Sparrow Jack by Mordicai Gerstein (2003)
  When the Wolves Returned by Dorothy Hinshaw Patent (2008)

- Description (these texts are from a list compiled by Carol Simoneau)—

  A Dragon in the Sky by Laurence Pringle (2001)
  Crocodiles and Alligators by Seymour Simon (2001)
  Feathers by Dorothy Patent (1992)
  It Could Still Be a Bird by Allan Fowler (1990)
  Safari Beneath the Sea by Diane Swanson (1994)
  What the Moon Is Like by Franklyn Branley (1986)

- Homework and Practice—Create and post a class list of signal words for each structure—comparison and contrast, cause and effect, sequence, problem and solutions, and description. Scan current texts and trade books or others provided to begin your list. Add to the list as you read. There are several words you can add. As words are added to the list, write sample sentences for each structure and discuss in class how each new sentence fits the structure. (RLST.6-8.5, SL.6.1)

- Compare and Contrast—
    - Similar
    - Different
    - Either, or
    - Compared to
    - However
    - In contrast
- Cause and Effect—
    - Because
    - As a result of
    - If/then
    - Since
    - Therefore
    - Due to
- Sequence—
    - First, second, etc.
    - Next
    - Before
    - Finally
    - During
- Problem and Solution—
    - Possible answer
    - A problem is
    - A solution is
    - Is solved by
- Description—
    - The characteristics are
    - For example
    - For instance
    - Contains
    - To illustrate
- Homework and Practice—Create and share graphic organizers to illustrate each type of structure. Use a short nonfiction text to help create your graphic organizer. Create story maps for multiple structure texts, Venn diagrams for compare and contrast, cause and effect organizers, problem and solution frames, and tables or charts for descriptions. (RLST.6-8.5)

- Homework and Practice—Use advance organizers to introduce new content, analyze the organizational structure and aid in understanding of the topic (see appendix F). (RLST.6-8.5)
- Homework and Practice—Use SQRRR before a new chapter or unit of content (see appendix A). (RLST.6-8.5)
- Compare and Contrast—Before students can determine author's purpose to explain or describe procedures or experiments, they should know the differences and components of each. In small groups create a three-circle Venn diagram to illustrate the similarities and differences in explanations, procedures, and experiments. Groups should then share their findings with each other and misconceptions should be corrected. (RLST.6-8.6, SL.6.1)
- Compare and Contrast—Read selections representative of author's purposes to explain something, describe a procedure and discuss an experiment. Write an essay that compares and contrasts the topics and why the authors chose to write the selections in the manner in which they were written. Edit writing for grammar and mechanics. (RLST.6-8.6, WHST.6-8.2, L.6.1, .6.2, L.6.3)
- Summaries—Read a nonfiction selection and write a summary of the author's explanation, description of a procedure, or discussion of an experiment. (RLST.6-8.6, WHST.6-8.2)
- Homework and Practice—Read an article or other selection that provides an explanation. Discuss with a partner or write an essay to describe what is explained, what new information was learned, how you can use the information, and identify any new questions you now have. Who would benefit most from the explanation? Does the author try to convince or persuade you about something connected to the explanation? Explain your reasoning and cite textual evidence when necessary. (RLST.6-8.6, RLST.6-8.1, WHST.6-8.2, SL.6.1, L.6.1, L.6.2, L.6.3)
  - Create a graphic organizer to answer the questions and share it with a partner or the class instead of writing an essay.
- Homework and Practice—Read an article or other selection that describes a procedure. Discuss with a partner or write an essay to describe the focus of the procedure itself and what the author is trying to explain. Why does the author feel the need to describe the procedure? Who would benefit most from the description? Is the author's explanation of the procedure clear, or do you have new questions? Explain your reasoning and cite textual evidence when necessary. Edit writing for grammar and mechanics. (RLST.6-8.6, RLST.6-8.1, WHST.6-8.2, SL.6.1, L.6.1, L.6.2, L.6.3)
- Homework and Practice—Read an article or other selection that describes or discusses an experiment. Discuss with a partner or write an essay to identify the focus of the experiment and the au-

thor's reason for describing or discussing it. What is the author trying to teach you? How can you use the new information? Who would benefit most from the description of the experiment? What new questions do you have? Edit writing for grammar and mechanics. (RLST.6-8.6, RLST.6-8.1, WHST.6-8.2, SL.6.1, L.6.1, L.6.2, L.6.3)

- Nonlinguistic Representations—Individually or in small groups, students create tables, charts, graphs, models, or diagrams to represent quantitative or technical information presented in words found in science or technical subjects text. Students share representations with the class. (RLST.6-8.7, SL.6.1)

    - Add tables, charts, graphs, models, or diagrams to individual or group presentations.

- Take Notes—Create a class table or chart with four columns—one each for the name of the source (newspaper, magazine, editorial, letter to the editor, journal article, or textbook selection), facts, opinions, and reasoned judgments. As a class, look at various sources to determine the facts, opinions and reasoned judgments. Be able to justify how you classified the statement. Make selections from those listed or other grade-appropriate text. Please check sources for appropriateness prior to classroom use. (RLHS.6-8.8, SL.6.1)

    www.dogonews.com/category/science
    http://eurekalert.org/kidsnews
    info@nanooze.org
    http://kids.nationalgeographickids.com/kids/stories
    www.odysseymagazine.com
    www.sciencecastle.com/sc/index.php/home/science_news
    www.sciencenews.org
    www.student.societyforscience.org
    http://teacher.scholastic.com/activities/scholasticnews
    www.timeforkids.com/news-archive/science

- Compare and Contrast—Conduct research on a topic of interest, researching reading texts, experiments (where applicable), simulations, videos and multimedia sources on the same topic. Take notes, remembering to add citations to the notes as you go for future reference. Create a graphic organizer to organize your thoughts. Share your organizer with a partner and your presentation plan. Consider the suggestions of your peers. Compare and contrast the information from your reading text to two other sources. How is the information alike? Different? What did you learn from each source you didn't learn from the other sources? Is there a difference in the way the information was presented in each source? Do all sources present facts and reasoned judgments or do any sources present opinions? (RLST.6-8.9, RLST.6-8.1, RLST.6-8.8, WHST.6-8.2, SL.6.1, L.6.1, L.6.2, L.6.3)

- Suggested Resources—(always check websites prior to use)

    Mysteries of Antiquity: Lessons to Engage Middle School Students in Ancient/Medieval History by Max Fischer (2001)
    Short Role-Playing Simulations for Middle School World History by Richard Di Giacomo (2012)
    www.americaslibrary.gov—Learn about America's story
    www.archives.gov/research—Research the National Archives for photos and documents
    www.brighthubeducation.com/middle-school-history-lessons/110630-europe-in-the-middle-ages-teaching-ideas—Middle school students learn about life in Medieval Europe
    www.csun.edu/~hcedu013/onlineactivities.html—Online simulation activities
    www.ebscohost.com/public/science-reference-center—Simulations, videos and more
    www.kidzsearch.com—Safe, family-friendly search engine for kids
    www.middleschool.net/curlink/science/scimain.htm—Middle school science activities site
    http://msms.ehe.ous.edu/tag/simulations—Quality resources for math and science simulations
    www.nationalparkservice.org—Research the National Park Service to find out information on monuments and other information about the states
    www.techtrekers.com/webquests/social.html—Social studies and science simulations

- Nonlinguistic Presentations—Create a model, diorama, display, collage, or scrapbook to represent information gained from reading texts, experiments, simulations, videos, and multimedia sources on the same topic. (RLST.6-8.9, RLST.6-8.10)

ELEVEN

Grade 6 Strategies and Activities for Writing in History, Social Studies, Science, and Technical Subjects

Choose literary or informational text from Grades 6–8 text exemplars selections or other appropriate grade level selections. Grades 6–8 text exemplars are noted with an (EX). The standards are grade-span in nature, but the text suggestions and activities are on a Grade 6 level.

- Homework and Practice—Write an argument to criticize a resource you used in researching a topic; offer two to three ways to improve the resource. Support the claims with reasoned logic. Be specific as to how and why the resource was worthy of criticism. Did you find incorrect data? Did the author have knowledge of the topic? Write and edit the argument for grammar and mechanics. Prepare to share the argument with the class. (WHST.6-8.1, WHST.6-8.4, WHST.6-8.5, WHST.6-8.8, WHST.6-8.9, WHST.6-8.10, SL.6.1, L.6.1, L.6.2, L.6.3)
- Homework and Practice—Think about all the environments you have studied this year. What is the best place for you live? Select where you would most like to live and write an argument defending your choice, supporting your claim with logical reasoning and relevant, accurate data and evidence. Use appropriate words, phrases and clauses for cohesion. Maintain a formal style and provide a concluding statement. Edit your argument for grammar and mechanic. Present your argument to the class. (WHST.6-8.1, WHST.6-8.4, WHST.6-8.5, WHST.6-8.6, WHST.6-8.8, WHST.6-8.9, WHST.6-8.10, SL.6.1, L.6.1, L.6.2, L.6.3)
- Homework and Practice—Write a variety of arguments on discipline-specific content supporting your claims with logical reason-

ing and relevant, accurate data and evidence. Use appropriate words, phrases, and clauses for cohesion. Maintain a formal style and provide a concluding statement. Edit your argument for grammar and mechanic. You may be asked to present your argument to the class. (WHST.6-8.1, WHST.6-8.4, WHST.6-8.5, WHST.6-8.6, WHST.6-8.8, WHST.6-8.9, WHST.6-8.10, SL.6.1, L.6.1, L.6.2, L.6.3)

- Topic suggestions—
    - Fast foods are/are not a nutritious source for kids.
    - Junk food sales should/should not be banned.
    - Our dependence on computers now, including smartphones, tablets, and laptops, will/will not be a hindrance to oral communication in the future.
    - Advertisers should/should not be allowed to target children in their ads.
    - Mass media does/does not influence me.
    - With the ever-present mass media and its potential to shape opinions and positions of young adults, should eighteen-year-olds continue to have the right to vote?
    - I am/am not swayed on issues by what I hear and see on social media.
    - What are the pros and cons of sixth graders using cell phones?
    - Video games have a positive/negative effect on kids and young adults.
    - Schools should/should not provide laptop computers for all students in middle school.
- Compare and Contrast—Consider arguments or informative or explanatory presentations and your topic. Compare and contrast some aspect of your topic with that of another topic in an essay. If the topics are the same, what is similar and different? If the topics are different, how is yours similar? Create an outline to organize thoughts. Seek guidance and support from peers and adults. Write and edit your essay for grammar and mechanics. Use technology to produce and publish writing. (WHST.6-8.2, WHST.6-8.4, WHST.6-8.5, WHST.6-8.6, WHST.6-8.9, WHST.6-8.10, SL.6.1, SL.6.6, L.6.1, L.6.2, L.6.3)
- Compare and Contrast—Choose two historical advertisements for similar products. You can choose from Ad*Access or other appropriate sources. Write an essay to compare and contrast the two ads. What was the author's purpose and how do you know? Based on the loaded words, which product would you buy and why? Did the author succeed in her purpose? Edit for grammar and mechanics.

(WHST.6-8.2, WHST.6-8.4, WHST.6-8.5, WHST.6-8.6, WHST.6-8.9, L.6.1, L.6.2, L.6.3)
- Homework and Practice—Conduct research to learn about a scientist, inventor, historical personality, or someone you've read about in a technical subject. Pretend you are that person and you are going to be interviewed for a newspaper from your time period. What would you want to be asked and how would you respond? Write a narrative interview based on informative texts using transitions, precise language, and formal style. Share your "interviews" with the class. Edit for grammar and mechanics. (WHST.6-8.2, WHST.6-8.4, WHST.6-8.6, WHST.6-8.8, WHST.6-8.9, WHST.6-8.10, SL.6.1, L.6.1, L.6.2, L.6.3)
    - Possible topics—
        Virginia Apgar
        Archimedes
        John J. Audubon
        Benjamin Banneker
        Clara Barton
        Alexander Graham Bell
        Elizabeth Blackwell
        George Washington Carver
        Anders Celsius
        Jacques Cousteau
        Marie Curie
        Leonardo DaVinci
        George Eastman
        Thomas Alva Edison
        Albert Einstein
        Henry Ford
        Benjamin Franklin
        Bill Gates
        Charles Goodyear
        Edwin Hubble
        Howard Hughes
        Steve Jobs
        Isaac Newton
        Louis Pasteur
        Sally Ride
        Jonas Salk
        Eli Whitney
        Orville and Wilbur Wright
- Homework and Practice—Conduct research using multiple print and digital sources on a topic related to a technical subject and

write an informative or explanatory report or develop a project. Your teacher will give you specific criteria to follow. Choose from topics listed or other appropriate topics. Include quantitative or technical information in the form of a visual as well as a model, diorama, or other product that represents something about your topic. Edit your writing for grammar and mechanics. Use technology to produce and publish your writing. Share your report or project with the class. (WHST.6-8.2, WHST.6-8.4, WHST.6-8.5, WHST.6-8.6, WHST.6-8.8, WHST.6-8.9, WHST.6-8.10, SL.6.1, L.6.1, L.6.2, L.6.3)

- Topic suggestions —
  - History of the computer — the development of hardware and software
  - The development of computer games
  - Pioneers in computing
  - Women in the computing industry
  - Timeline of the Internet
  - Computer terms dictionary
  - Create a web page
  - How have advances in science and technology in the last five years affected each other and society?
- Analyze and explain how specific technological solutions may impact the environment.

  Solar energy
  Wind energy
  Nuclear energy
  Geothermal energy
  Green technology

- Identify current investigations and technological advances in the news. Choose one and determine the benefit or risks to health or society or the environment.
- How have building and construction methods changed over the years?
- How do modern day buildings withstand earthquakes?
- How much time do we as sixth graders spend with technology? Survey sixth grade students. Document the time students spend using various devices. Which is used most and for what purpose? Which is used least and why? How much time is spent using technology during the school day? School evening? Weekends? Is technology used too much or not enough or for the appropriate and beneficial reasons?

- Homework and Practice—Conduct research using multiple print and digital sources on a topic related to a science or technical career and write an informative or explanatory report. Your teacher will give you specific criteria to follow. Choose from topics listed or other appropriate topics. Address the career prep courses, job description, day-to-day duties, salary or pay, and where in the country or world the career opportunities are the best. What is one interesting fact that you would not associate with your topic? Include quantitative or technical information in the form of a visual as well as a model, diorama, or other product that represents something about your topic. Edit your writing for grammar and mechanics. Use technology to produce and publish your writing. Share your report or project with the class. (WHST.6-8.2, WHST.6-8.4, WHST.6-8.5, WHST.6-8.6, WHST.6-8.8, WHST.6-8.9, WHST.6-8.10, SL.6.1, L.6.1, L.6.2, L.6.3)
    - As a post-writing activity, complete a "I think I'd like to be a . . ." T-chart that lists the pros and cons for the career you chose. Share the chart with a partner or the class after your presentation.
    - If possible, interview or job-shadow someone in the career field you chose to gain personal insight to that career.
- Homework and Practice—Conduct research using multiple print and digital sources on a topic related to history and social studies and write an informative or explanatory report. Your teacher will give you specific criteria to follow. Choose from topics listed or other appropriate topics. Include a model, diorama, illustration, or other product that represents something about your topic. Edit your writing for grammar and mechanics. Use technology to produce and publish your writing. Share your report or project with the class. (WHST.6-8.2, WHST.6-8.4, WHST.6-8.5, WHST.6-8.6, WHST.6-8.8, WHST.6-8.9, WHST.6-8.10, SL.6.1, L.6.1, L.6.2, L.6.3)
    - Topic suggestions—
        Choose a specific battle of the Civil War
        Egyptian pyramids
        History of the Colony of Massachusetts
        History of the Lost Colony of Roanoke
        History of the Colony of Rhode Island
        Salem Witch trials
        Mathew Brady
        Louisiana Purchase
        Marco Polo
        Revolutionary War
        Hammurabi

Aztec Code
Christopher Columbus
Immigration today
Women of World War II
The Abolitionist Movement
The Gold Rush

- Homework and Practice—Pretend you are a scientist, inventor, or historical personality and write a letter to your biographer. Let the biographer know how pleased or displeased you are about the biography. Choose one or two of your most important lifetime events and tell the story "no one ever knew" about the events. Give or deny the biographer the permission to publish the new information and explain your reasons for giving or denying permission. Use appropriate friendly letter format and edit your writing for grammar and mechanics. Share your letter with the class. (WHST.6-8.2, WHST.6-8.4, WHST.6-8.6, WHST.6-8.8, WHST.6-8.9, WHST.6-8.10, SL.6.1, L.6.1, L.6.2, L.6.3)
- Homework and Practice—Select a paragraph written in one organizational structure and rewrite it in another organizational structure. What changes did you have to make with regard to the information? What other changes did you have to make? (WHST.6-8.2, RLHS.6-8.5, RLST.6-8.5)
- Summaries—After selecting a topic and conducting initial research, write summaries about what you would most like to learn or know about the topic. (WHST.6-8.7)
- Take Notes—Identify five to ten new words or phrases related to your topic. Cite the page numbers so you can refer to them later. Define the words or phrases, determine the part of speech, the root word, the affixes, and word origin. Try to use the words and phrases in your writing as it was used in context in your research. (WHST.6-8.7, RHST.6-8.1, RLST.6-8.1)
- Take Notes—Identify sources for research and write down the bibliographic information for use later. (WHST.6-8.7)
- Hypothesize and Test—Create a hypothesis worksheet (see appendix D). Complete the worksheet to help you focus on your topic and develop your hypothesis. (WHST.6-8.7)
- Questions—When you begin research, consider a variety of questions. (WHST.6-8.7)
  - What are five to ten questions you most would like to answer about your topic?
  - What are three to five specific sources you can use to learn about your topic and why?
  - What are five to ten ways you can share information about your topic?

- How would you divide your topics into subtopics?
- Is there someone you can interview and what questions would you ask?

- Questions—When conducting research, ask and find answers to a variety of relevant questions based on stem statements in appendix C. (WHST.6-8.7)
- Homework and Practice—Conduct short research projects to answer questions using a variety of sources and generating additional focused questions that allow for continued exploration. Choose from topics listed next or others supplied by your teacher. Consider questions you would most like to answer through your research on a topic. Choose one question and conduct research to answer that question. Present your question and answer in the form of a press conference or news story to the class. End your presentation with additional questions that inspire continued exploration of the topic. (WHST.6-8.7, WHST.6-8.2, WHST.6-8.4, WHST.6-8.5, WHST.6-8.6, WHST.6-8.8, WHST.6-8.9, WHST.6-8.10, SL.6.1, L.6.1, L.6.2, L.6.3)
    - Topic suggestions—
        - How do you create a PowerPoint presentation?
        - How do you use Windows Movie Maker?
        - What is iMovie?
        - What is Keynote?
        - How do you use Appleworks Slideshow?
        - What is HyperStudio?
        - What is MediaBlender?
        - How does technology improve the classroom today? Interview a teacher, parent, and student.
- Homework and Practice—Practice writing hypothesis questions and "if/then" statements (see appendix D). (WHST.6-8.7)

Appendix A: Summary Frames

Narrative Frame

1. Who are the main characters and what are they like?
2. Where and when does the story take place?
3. What prompted the action in the story?
4. How did the characters express their feelings?
5. What did the main characters decide to do? If they set a goal, what was it?
6. How did the main characters try to accomplish their goal?
7. What were the consequences?

Definition Frame

1. What is being defined?
2. To which general category does the item belong?
3. What characteristics separate the item from other things in the general category?
4. What are some different types or classes or the item being defined?

Problem-Solution Frame

1. What is the problem?
2. What is a possible solution?
3. What is another possible solution?
4. Which solution has the best chance of succeeding?

Argumentation Frame

1. What information is presented that leads to a claim?
2. What is the basic statement or claim that is the focus of the information?
3. What examples or explanations are presented to support this claim?
4. What concessions are made about the claim?

Somebody-Wanted-But-So-Then Frame

Somebody: identify the character
Wanted: state the goal of the character
But: state the problem/conflict
So Then: state the resolution

SQRRR Frame

> Survey: Read and record the main titles and subtitles from the chapter sections
> Question: Turn topic headings into questions—who, what, where, when, why, and how
> Read: Read the text to answer the questions you just asked, taking notes as you go
> Recite: Answer the questions you asked orally and in your own words
> Review: Write a short summary that answers each question you asked

Bio-poem

> Line 1: Person's first name
> Line 2: Four adjectives that describe the person
> Line 3: Likes (name three things) example: Likes dogs, cats, turtles
> Line 4: Gives (name three things) example: Gives hope, comfort, kisses
> Line 5: Fears (name three things) example: Fears strangers, new places, photographers
> Line 6: Would like to see (name three things) example: Would like to see Paris, Atlanta, tigers
> Line 7: Lives (name the city or place)
> Line 8: Person's last name

Appendix B: Position Paper Format

Introductory Paragraph— State your thesis or argument (this is your view of the issue) Introduce the topic Use organized structure	This paper will argue that . . . (thesis)
Premise 1— Give a single concept, idea, body of evidence Include facts, evidence and support Include your own analysis and interpretation	(Restate your thesis) because . . .
Premise 2— Give a single concept, idea, body of evidence Include facts, evidence and support Include your own analysis and interpretation	(Restate your thesis) because . . .
Premise 3— Give a single concept, idea, body of evidence Include facts, evidence and support Include your own analysis and interpretation	(Restate your thesis) because . . .
Concluding Paragraph— Restate your thesis Restate each premise Give no new information *(You can begin your conclusion with words such as finally, in a word, in brief, in conclusion, in the end, in the final analysis, on the whole, thus, to conclude, to summarize, in sum, in summary)	In conclusion*, (thesis). First, because (premise 1). Second, because (premise 2). Third, because (premise 3).

Appendix C: Stem Questions

Post these stem questions and statements with your Verbs to Question list. Refer to both in classroom instruction as you work toward implementing higher-order questions in classroom instruction.

- Can you make a distinction between . . . ?
- Can you recall, name, select, list . . . ?
- Compare two like characters, people, events, places, causes-effects.
- Could you explain your reasons?
- Define _____ using context clues.
- Describe the relationship between . . . ?
- Do you agree with the actions or outcome . . . ?
- Explain how . . .
- Explain the meaning of . . .
- Explain which clues from the text helped you understand the meaning.
- Give an example of . . .
- How did the title of _____ give a clue to the action/event that followed?
- How does _____? Support your answer.
- How does _____ compare/contrast with _____ ?
- How is _____ related to _____ ?
- How would you classify, compare, contrast . . . ?
- How would things be different if . . . ?
- Identify the characteristics of . . .
- List _____ major events in order.
- List the differences/similarities in . . .
- Show or explain the role of . . .
- What examples can you find . . . ?
- What facts or ideas show . . . ?
- What ideas can you add to . . . ?
- What criteria might you use to judge or evaluate . . . ?
- What evidence supports . . . ?
- What is your opinion of . . . ?
- What are the characteristics of . . . ?
- What approach or strategy could you use to . . . ?
- What could happen if . . . ?
- What might be the result of . . . ?

- What might you infer from ... ?
- What conclusions might be drawn from ... ?
- What ideas or details can you add to ... ?
- What was the most important event ... ?
- What would be an example ... ?
- What would be the benefit(s) of ... ?
- Who, what, when, where, why ... ?
- Why do you think ... ?
- Why was the setting important?

Appendix D: Hypothesis Worksheet

State your topic.
　　The topic I am researching is:

Write the question.
　　The question I want to answer is:

State what you already know about the topic.
　　I know these three things about my topic:

　　1.
　　2.
　　3.

Conduct research using various sources to find important information about your topic.
　　New information on my topic includes:

The hypothesis is _____.
　　What will the answer to your question be? Make a prediction in the form of an if/then statement.

Appendix E: Primary Source Analysis

Directions: Analyze and evaluate primary documents and record your information here. You may not use all questions for all documents.

Title:

Date of the document:

General subject in the document:

Type of document:

Who created the document?

Who was the intended audience?

Why was the document written?

What is the author's point of view?

What specific examples of bias do you find?

How is the author connected to the document?

Is there a similar document that confirms or contradicts information in this primary source?

What is it and what information is confirmed or contradicted?

What are two new things you learned?

Look up and define any new terms or phrases.

What does the document help you to see about life or the culture of the time?

What new questions do you have now?

Appendix F: Sample Grade 6 Advance Organizers

Create advance organizers for new stories, dramas, poems, or new informational text and share with students prior to reading.
Use graphic organizers like

- KWL charts
- Flow charts
- Outlines
- Webs
- SQRRR strategies

- 5W and How
- Timelines
- Narrative frames
- Venn diagrams

Use expository advance organizers to describe the new content to be learned. Here is an example:

Today we begin to read about a key figure in the Civil War by reading the book Lincoln's Last Days: The Shocking Assassination That Changed America Forever *by Bill O'Reilly and Dwight Zimmerman (2012). As a class we will read and discuss the text looking at the beginning of the war, the assassination conspiracy, the last days of Lincoln's life, and the chase for the assassins.*

As we read, we will determine the central idea of the text and in class discussions we will look at how the idea is conveyed through the use of details. You will individually analyze and describe in detail how a key individual, event, or idea is introduced, illustrated, and elaborated in the text. You may choose to create a character map, timeline, concept web, or other graphic organizer. You will also want to cite textual evidence to support you analysis of what the text says and infers.

Finally, you will write an informative/explanatory essay to describe the author's point of view or purpose in the text and explain how it is conveyed in the text. You will introduce and develop your topic using relevant facts, definitions, details, and quotations. Use appropriate transitions and precise language and a concluding statement. (RI.6.1, RI.6.2, RI.6.3, RI.6.5, W.6.2, W.6.4, W.6.5, W.6.10, SL.6.1, L.6.1, L.6.2, L.6.3, L.6.6)

A narrative advance organizer could look like this:

As you know you are about to read the book Lincoln's Last Days: The Shocking Assassination That Changed America Forever *by Bill O'Reilly and Dwight Zimmerman (2012). When we read the book last year, my students were able to attend a Lincoln Days event. The event was very useful to help explain everyday life in Lincoln's time. It helped students to see that life was very different then.*

Students were able to participate in pioneer games like corn shelling, tug of war, egg toss, horseshoe toss and a bucket brigade. They also took part in the Lincoln scavenger hunt where they had to look at various sculptures and monuments for information to answer the questions on the scavenger hunt.

Other highlights included the parade, displays of quilts and various pioneer tools, professional rail splitting, and they even got to pretend to "pack a wagon." Students selected items that would be needed for the journey west, but were limited to a one-thousand-pound capacity. It was really funny what some chose to take. The best part last year was watching the Civil War reenactors fight a battle with guns, horses, and end even cannons.

My surprise for you this year is that you not only get to attend a Lincoln Days event, but we are also going to get a private screening of the movie Killing Lincoln, *adapted from the O'Reilly book by Erik Jendresen. We will then compare and contrast in class discussions the experience of reading the text to watching the film. (RL.6.7, SL.6.1)*

To practice skimming, use the book *DK Biography: Abraham Lincoln: A Photographic Story of a Life* by Tanya Lee Stone (2005). Use the information to create an outline or a concept web.

Appendix G: Sample Parent Letter

Date:

Dear Parent or Guardian:
   Today we worked on the following skills or concepts in class:

   1.
   2.
   3.

Please let your son or daughter share with you the above skills or concepts as he or she practices them at home. As you share this time with your child, it would be helpful if you would look for the following as your child practices:

Your child and I appreciate your time as you help him or her achieve success through practice.

Sincerely,

Appendix H: Products and Performances

The following list of products and performances gives you suggestions for alternative homework assignments, projects, or performance assessments. You will find activities to address a wide range of grade levels and student abilities suitable for the implementation of CCSS.

Acrostic poems	Directions
Advertisements	Displays
Art product	Dramatizations
Artifact analysis	Drawings
Attribute chart	Essays
Audio tape	Experiment
Autobiography	Eyewitness report
Banner	Fable
Board games	Fairy tale
Book cover	Family tree
Bookmark	Film critique
Brochure	Flags
Bulletin board	Flowchart
Captions	Foods
Cartoons	Forum on an issue
CD covers	Game
Characterizations	Glossary
Character study	Graph
Chart	Greeting card
Choral reading	Haiku
Clay sculpture	Illustrated story
Collage	Illustrations
Collections	Interview
Creative writings	Invitation
Crosswords	Journals
Demonstrations	Learning center
Diagrams	Letter to the editor
Diary	Letter—personal
Dictionary	Logo
Diorama	Logs (reading)

Lyrics
Magazine articles
Map
Mind map
Mobile
Model
Montage
Mosaic
Movie clip
Mural
Museum exhibit
News report
Newsletter
Note cards
Oral presentations
Outline
Painting
Pamphlet
Panel discussion
Pantomime
Papier-mache
Paraphrase
Pen-pal project
Photo album
Photo essay
Picture story
Plan
Play
Poetry
Poetry anthology
Poll
Portfolio
Position paper
Poster
Pottery
Presentation
Press conference
Project cube
Prototype
Puppet
Puppet show
Puzzle

Questionnaire
Q & A session
Quiz show
Rap
Reader's theater
Rebus story
Recipe
Recipe book
Recommendation
Report
Research paper
Response paper
Riddle
Role-play
Schedule
Science fiction
Scrapbook
Script
Sculpture
Shoebox collection
Short story
Signs
Skit
Slide show
Slogan
Song
Speeches
Spelling bee
Sports story
Storyboard
Story poem
Story map
Summary
Survey
Tables
Tall tale
Timeline
Tri-fold
Venn diagram
Videotape
Weather report

Appendix I: Verbs to Question

The verbs listed here can be found on many different lists and are generally broken down into separate categories. It may be more useful to categorize them into just two alphabetized lists. The first list consists of verbs that are considered by most teachers to be lower-level recall verbs. The second list consists of verbs that are generally considered higher-order verbs.

LOWER-ORDER VERBS

add	infer
ask	interpret
choose	know
classify	label
compare	list
conclude	listen
contrast	locate
convert	match
count	memorize
define	name
demonstrate	observe
describe	omit
determine	outline
differentiate	paraphrase
discover	predict
discuss	read
display	recall
distinguish	recite
estimate	recognize
explain	record
express	relate
extend	repeat
find	rephrase
generalize	report
how	restate
identify	retell
illustrate	retrieve

review
rewrite
say
select
show
spell
state
summarize
tell

trace
translate
underline
what
when
where
which
who
why

HIGHER-ORDER VERBS

adapt
agree
analyze
apply
appraise
argue
arrange
assemble
assess
assume
award
build
calculate
categorize
change
classify
code
combine
compare
compile
compose
compute
conclude
connect
construct
contrast
convince
create
criticize
critique
debate

deduce
deduct
defend
delete
demonstrate
derive
design
determine
develop
diagnose
diagram
differentiate
discover
discriminate
dispute
dissect
distinguish
divide
draw
editorialize
elaborate
employ
examine
execute
experiment
explain
explore
formulate
hypothesize
illustrate
imagine

improve
infer
integrate
interpret
interview
invent
judge
justify
make up
manipulate
maximize
measure
minimize
model
modify
operate
order
organize
originate
paint
participate
perceive
perform
plan
practice
predict
prepare
pretend
prioritize
produce
propose
prove
rank

rate
rearrange
reason
recommend
reconstruct
record
relate
reorganize
revise
role-play
rule on
select
separate
sketch
solve
specify
state a rule
substitute
suggest
summarize
support
survey
teach
test
theorize
transfer
uncover
use
validate
value
verify
visualize
write

References

Anderson, T. H., & Armbruster, B. B. (1986). *The value of taking notes during lectures* (Tech. Rep. No. 374). Cambridge, MA: Bolt, Beranek and Newman and Center for the Study of Reading, Urbana, Illinois. (ERIC Document Reproduction Service No. ED 277 996).

Anderson, V., & Hidi, S. (1988/1989). Teaching students to summarize. *Educational Leadership, 46,* 26–28.

Armstrong, T. (2006). The best schools: How human development research should inform educational practice. Alexandria, VA: Association for Supervision and Curriculum Development.

Bond, G. W., & Smith, G. J. (1966). Homework in the elementary school. *The National Elementary School Principal, 45*(3), 46–50.

Bransford, J., Brown, A., & Cocking, R. (1999). *How people learn: Brain, mind, experience and school.* Washington, DC: National Academy Press.

Brookbank, D., Grover, S., Kullberg, K., & Strawser, C. (1999). Improving student achievement through organization of student learning. Chicago: Master's Action Research Project, Saint Xavier University and IRI/Skylight. (ERIC Document Reproduction Service No. ED 435094)

Cooper, H. (1989). Synthesis of research on homework. *Educational Leadership, 47*(3), 85–91.

Dale, E. (1969). *Audio-visual methods in teaching* (3rd ed.). Hinsdale, IL: Dryden Press.

Davis, O. L., & Tinsley, D. (1967). Cognitive objectives revealed by classroom questions asked by social studies teachers and their pupils. *Peabody Journal of Education, 44,* 21–26.

Duke study: Homework helps students succeed in school, as long as there isn't too much. (2006, March 7). Retrieved from http://today.duke.edu/2006/03/homework.html.

Education Northwest. (2005). *Focus on effectiveness: Integrating technology into research-based strategies.* Retrieved from Northwest Educational Technology Consortium website: http://www.netc.org/focus/.

Fillipone, M. (1998). *Questioning at the elementary level.* (Master's thesis). Kean University. (ERIC Document Reproduction Service No. ED 417 431).

Fisher, D., & Frey, N. (2007). *Checking for understanding: Formative Assessment techniques for your classroom.* Alexandria, VA: Association for Supervision and Curriculum Development.

Fowler, T. W. (1975, March). An investigation of the teacher behavior of wait-time during an inquiry science lesson. Paper presented at the annual meeting of the National Association for Research in Science Teaching, Los Angeles. (ERIC Document Reproduction Service No. ED 108 872).

Janel W. (2009, October 18). Generating and testing hypotheses is not just for science [McRel blog]. Retrieved from http://mcrel.typepad.com/mcrel_blog/2009/06/generating-and-testing-hypotheses-is-not-just-for-science.html?cid=6a010536aec25c970b0115724ac441970b.

Johnson, D. W., & Johnson, R. T. (1999). Learning together and alone: Cooperative, competitive, and individualistic learning. Boston, MA: Allyn and Bacon.

Jones, F. A. (1908). *Thomas Alva Edison: Sixty years of an inventors life.* New York: Thomas Y. Crowell.

Kagan, S., & Kagan, M. (1997). *Kagan cooperative learning smart card*. San Clemente, CA: Kagan Publishing.

Keith, T. Z., & Cool, V. A. (1992). Teaching models of school learning: Effects of quality instruction, motivation, academic coursework, and homework on academic achievement. *School Psychology Quarterly, 7*, 209–226.

Kuhn, M. (2009, June 22). Generating and testing hypotheses is not just for science [McRel blog]. Retrieved from http://mcrel.typepad.com/mcrel_blog/2009/06/generating-and-testing-hypotheses-is-not-just-for-science.html?cid=6a010536aec25c970b0115724ac441970b.

Lavoie, D. R., & Good, R. (1998). The nature and use of prediction skills in biological computer simulation. *Journal of Research in Science Teaching, 25*, 334–360.

Lawson, A. E. (1998). A better way to teach biology. *The American Biology Teacher, 50*, 266–278.

Leach, S. (2010, February 2). Generating and testing hypotheses is not just for science [McRel blog]. Retrieved from http://mcrel.typepad.com/mcrel_blog/2009/06/generating-and-testing-hypotheses-is-not-just-for-science.html?cid=6a010536aec25c970b0115724ac441970b.

Lehrer, R., & Chazen, D. (1998). *Designing learning environments for developing understanding of geometry and space*. Mahwah, NJ: Erlbaum.

Markman, A. B., & Gentner, D. (1996). Commonalities and differences in similarity comparisons. *Memory and Cognition, 24*(2), 235–249.

Marzano, R. J., Pickering, D. J., & Pollock, J. (2001). *Classroom instruction that works: Research-based strategies for increasing student achievement*. Alexandria, VA: Association for Supervision and Curriculum Development.

McGarvey, B. (2007, January). The war on homework. *Education Update, 49* (1), 6.

Meyer, B. F., & Freedle, R. O. (1984). Effects of discourse type on recall. *American Education Research Journal, 21*, 121–144.

National Council of Teachers of Mathematics. (2000). Principles and standards for school mathematics. Reston, VA: Author.

National Governors Association Center for Best Practices, Council of Chief School Officers. (2010). Common core state standards for language arts. Washington, DC: Author

Pennsylvania Department of Education. (1973). *Study on homework: Homework policies in the public schools of Pennsylvania and selected states in the nation*. Harrisburg, PA: Author.

Redfield, D. L., & Rousseau, E. W. (1981). A meta-analysis of experimental research on teacher questioning behavior. *Review of Educational Research, 51*(2), 237–245.

Strang, R. (1975). *Homework: What research says to teachers* (Series). Washington, DC: National Education Association.

Vatterott, C. (2009). *Rethinking homework: Best practices that support diverse needs*. Alexandria, VA: Association for Supervision and Curriculum Development.

White, B. Y., & Frederickson, J. R. (1998). Inquiry, modeling, and metacognition: Making science accessible to all students. *Cognition and Instruction, 16*(1), 3–117.

About the Author

Michelle Manville taught elementary and middle school for sixteen years in Missouri and served as the K–12 curriculum director for her district for ten years. She also served on many local and state curriculum committees and was a Missouri Select Teacher for Regional Resources curriculum trainer for two years.

Since her retirement in 2010, Manville has written five resource books for teachers that identify specific, effective research-based strategies and activities. *Common Core State Standards for Grades K–1: Language Arts Instructional Strategies and Activities, Common Core State Standards for Grades 2–3: Language Arts Instructional Strategies and Activities, Common Core State Standards for Grades 4–5: Language Arts Instructional Strategies and Activities, Common Core State Standards for Grade 6: Language Arts Instructional Strategies and Activities,* and *Common Core State Standards for Grade 7: Language Arts Instructional Strategies and Activities* are available now. Grade 8 will be available soon.

Manville currently spends her free time with her husband on the family farm or at their home on Lake of the Ozarks.

www.ingramcontent.com/pod-product-compliance
Lightning Source LLC
Chambersburg PA
CBHW030142240426
43672CB00005B/235